I0797835

The Qur'an has it all

How the Qur'an Answers All of Life's Questions

HAIFAA YOUNIS

The Qur'an has it all

First published in England by
Kube Publishing Ltd
Markfield Conference Centre
Ratby Lane, Markfield
Leicestershire, LE67 9SY
United Kingdom

Tel: +44 (0) 1530 249230
Website: www.kubepublishing.com
Email: info@kubepublishing.com

 Cataloguing-in-Publication Data is available from the British Library

Editor: Suma Din

Cover Design and typesetting: Quillspire

Printer: IMAK, Turkey

ISBN: 978-1-84774-257-5 Hardback

eISBN: 978-1-84774-258-2

CONTENTS

DEDICATION

To everyone who taught me how to read the Qur'an

Who taught me how to understand the Qur'an

Who helped me memorise the Qur'an

Above all, taught me and still teaching me how to live the Qur'an

INTRODUCTION

In the name of Allah ﷻ, The Most Merciful, the Most Compassionate.

All praise is for Allah ﷻ. We seek His Help and ask His Forgiveness. We seek refuge in Him from the evil of our own souls and from the wickedness of our deeds. Whomever Allah ﷻ guides, nothing can make him misguided, and whomever He leaves astray, nothing can guide him. I bear witness that no one has the right to be worshipped but Allah ﷻ, Who has no partner, and I bear witness that Muhammad ﷺ is His slave and His Messenger.

كِتَـٰبٌ أَنزَلْنَـٰهُ إِلَيْكَ مُبَـٰرَكٌ لِّيَدَّبَّرُوٓا۟ ءَايَـٰتِهِۦ وَلِيَتَذَكَّرَ أُو۟لُوا۟ ٱلْأَلْبَـٰبِ

This is a blessed Scripture which We sent down to you [Muhammad], for people to think about its messages, and for those with understanding to take heed.

(*Saad* 38:29)

Millions of believers read the Qur'an on a daily basis. The recitation of the Qur'an is in itself a highly rewardable act of worship, as established by *Rasul Allah* ﷺ when he said: "Whoever recites a letter from the Book of Allah will be credited with a good deed, and a good deed gets a ten-fold reward. I do not say that Alif-Lam-Mim is one letter, but Alif is a letter, Lam is a letter, and Mim is a letter." [At-Tirmidhi].

In addition to the benefit of reading the Qur'an, Allah ﷻ tells us its purpose is clear guidance, and a light to guide believers:

وَنَزَّلْنَا عَلَيْكَ ٱلْكِتَـٰبَ تِبْيَـٰنًا لِّكُلِّ شَىْءٍ وَهُدًى وَرَحْمَةً وَبُشْرَىٰ لِلْمُسْلِمِينَ

...We have sent the Scripture down to you explaining everything, and as guidance and mercy and good news to those who have submitted to Allah.

(*al-Nahl* 16:89)

At the heart of reading the Qur'an is engaging with its message; what is Allah ﷻ saying to humankind? What does He want you to gain from its message? Our daily life is fast-paced, full of distractions, and you may feel like you're being pulled in multiple directions. It is easy to feel lost, as many people do. And this feeling gives rise to many questions, such as: Why am I here? Where am I going? What is my purpose on earth? If you come to the Qur'an with these questions, you will find the answers there.

If you are worried, the Qur'an gives guidance on how to deal with this, as we are reminded:

وَنُنَزِّلُ مِنَ ٱلْقُرْءَانِ مَا هُوَ شِفَآءٌ وَرَحْمَةٌ لِّلْمُؤْمِنِينَ ۙ وَلَا يَزِيدُ ٱلظَّـٰلِمِينَ إِلَّا خَسَارًا

We send down the Qur'an as healing and mercy to those who believe; as for those who disbelieve, it only increases their loss.

(*Bani Isra'il* 17:82)

If you wonder where you came from; the Qur'an has an explanation. If you ponder about where are you going, the Qur'an provides direction for this life and the next. If you wonder what role Allah ﷻ wants women to have, the Qur'an covers this. What about the role of men, the role of parents, the rights of children? The Qur'an covers all these questions. What about subjects such as money or beauty? What does the Qur'an say about this life and the creation; the sun and moon? I can assure you, you will find answers as: The Qur'an Has It All.

This book is based on Jannah Institute's Ramadan series: *The Qu'ran Has It All.* Ramadan is the month of the Qur'an, when reading, reciting and contemplating its verses are prominent features. As people enjoy going to the masajid and listening to the Qur'an during night prayers, I delivered these episodes to connect us to what Allah ﷻ is teaching us through the wisdom of the *ayaat.*

May Allah ﷻ accept this deed as a *sadaqah jariyah* (continuous form of charity) that will benefit us and future generations.

اللَّهُمَّ اجْعَلِ الْقُرْآنَ رَبِيعَ قَلْبِي وَنُورَ صَدْرِي وَجَلَاءَ حُزْنِي وَذَهَابَ هَمِّي

O Allah, make the Qur'an the spring of my heart, the light of my chest, the remover of my sadness, and the banisher of my worries.

Amīn

Shaykha Haifaa Younis

June 2025

Chapter 01

WHY ARE WE HERE?

Why did Allah ﷻ put us on this Earth?

It is human nature to be curious and ask questions. When these questions come with the intention to understand and strengthen our faith, then we should look sincerely to the Qur'an and teachings of *Rasul Allah* ﷺ, for answers. One of the most common questions we ask ourselves and each other is, why did Allah ﷻ put us on this Earth? Why did he create us? As with all the questions we have, when we look in the Qur'an, we find the answer.

وَإِذْ قَالَ رَبُّكَ لِلْمَلَائِكَةِ إِنِّي جَاعِلٌ فِي الْأَرْضِ خَلِيفَةً ۖ قَالُوا أَتَجْعَلُ
فِيهَا مَن يُفْسِدُ فِيهَا وَيَسْفِكُ الدِّمَاءَ وَنَحْنُ نُسَبِّحُ بِحَمْدِكَ
وَنُقَدِّسُ لَكَ ۖ قَالَ إِنِّي أَعْلَمُ مَا لَا تَعْلَمُونَ

O Muhammad! When your Lord Allah said to the angels, Indeed, I will make upon this Earth a successor, an authoritative figure. Angels responded, will you place upon it one who causes corruption and sheds blood while we angels exalt you with praise and declare your perfection? Allah responded, Indeed, I know what you don't know.

(*al-Baqarah* 2:30)

This verse is the opening scene of human creation and explains the beginning of everything. We were not created yet, but we encounter the reason why we were put on Earth. Allah ﷻ has this discussion in the above verse with the supreme society of the angels, and had decided what He was going to put on this Earth. Rather than keeping Earth empty or filling it with angels, He planned to occupy it with human beings. In his infinite wisdom, He decided to hand over all the affairs in this Earth to human beings – as a *khalifa*-representative. The human being would be given the responsibility for Earth's destiny with the freedom to use, develop and transform everything, using the energy and resources to serve Allah ﷻ and to fulfill His orders. The purpose, we learn, of putting us on this Earth is actually this: to fulfill what Allah ﷻ wants from us.

What is a *khalifa*?

Scholars of the past explored this question: what does the word *Khalifa* really mean? If we look at the translation, *Khalifa* means a successor; someone from whom future generations will come and who will be a representative. You and I are representatives of Allah ﷻ.

This means Allah ﷻ wants to see everything He has described himself as, His names and beautiful attributes, reflected in our conduct. We know Allah ﷻ is *Rahim*, all Merciful, He wants to see *Rahmah*-mercy between us. Allah ﷻ is Forgiving, for example; He wants to see forgiveness amongst us.

In this verse in Surah *al-An'am*, The Livestock, we are told about our purpose as *Khalifa*:

وَهُوَ ٱلَّذِى جَعَلَكُمْ خَلَٰٓئِفَ ٱلْأَرْضِ وَرَفَعَ بَعْضَكُمْ فَوْقَ بَعْضٍ دَرَجَٰتٍ لِّيَبْلُوَكُمْ
فِى مَآ ءَاتَىٰكُمْ ۗ إِنَّ رَبَّكَ سَرِيعُ ٱلْعِقَابِ وَإِنَّهُۥ لَغَفُورٌ رَّحِيمٌۢ

And it is He who has made you successors upon the Earth and has raised some of you above others in degrees [of rank] that He may try you through what He has given you. Indeed, your Lord is swift in penalty; but indeed, He is Forgiving and Merciful.

(*al-An'am* 6: 165)

The great scholar Qurtubi explained a *Khalifa* as a representative who judges disputes that occur between people, forbidding them from injustice and sin. *Sayyidina Adam* ﵇ was the first *Khalifa* of Allah ﷻ and carried out His commands and prohibitions.

In another verse, Allah ﷻ explained why He put us on Earth. And this time He didn't use the word *Khalifa* when he answered this question in *Surah al-Dhariyat* -Scattering Winds:

وَمَا خَلَقْتُ ٱلْجِنَّ وَٱلْإِنسَ إِلَّا لِيَعْبُدُونِ

I did not create humans and jinns but to worship me.

(*al-Dhariyat* 51:56).

If we look at the word worship -*ibadah* does this suggest we are just supposed to be praying, fasting or reading the Qur'an and not doing anything else in this life? If we believe this is what 'worship' means, then we have made the definition of *ibadah*, very limited indeed. Allah ﷻ will not ask us to perform only this limited understanding of *ibadah*. We need to ask ourselves how we're going to be the human being He wants us to be, as a *Khalifa* to work and take care of the Earth?

Imam ibn Taymiyyah answers this with a beautiful description. He said every act the human being does, external or internal, an action or saying that is pleasing to Allah ﷻ and He loves – is *ibadah*-worship.

كُلّ ما يحِبُّهُ اللهُ ويَرْضَاهُ مِنَ الأقوالِ والأَعْمَالِ البَاطِنَةِ والظَّاهِرةِ

If we imagine, every word, every action, internal and external, that Allah ﷻ loves and is pleased with, is counted as *ibadah*, this has a profound effect on our understanding. He put us here to obey Him, say what pleases Him, do what pleases Him and stay away from what He dislikes. Only then, can we call ourselves a true *Khalifa* with an appreciation of our role.

Points to reflect on:

- Allah ﷻ created each of us for a reason, with a purpose on this Earth. If we ever feel lost, we can reflect on this and be reassured our being on Earth is *Al-Khaliq's* plan.

- The human being is held in high regard in Allah's ﷻ sight; this should not make us arrogant, but humble us, feeling grateful for His blessing.

- We are all children of Adam عليه السلام. His role of being a *khalifa* on this Earth is also our role. Are we truly fulfilling our role of being His representative?

- When we learn about *Sayyidina Adam* عليه السلام, we are learning about ourselves; evaluating our strengths and weaknesses will help us when we are tested.

- We are here to worship Allah ﷻ. How can we make our everyday activities into acts of worship?

هُوَ اللَّهُ الَّذِي لَا إِلَٰهَ إِلَّا هُوَ ۖ عَالِمُ الْغَيْبِ وَالشَّهَادَةِ ۖ هُوَ الرَّحْمَٰنُ الرَّحِيمُ ۝ هُوَ
اللَّهُ الَّذِي لَا إِلَٰهَ إِلَّا هُوَ الْمَلِكُ الْقُدُّوسُ السَّلَامُ الْمُؤْمِنُ الْمُهَيْمِنُ الْعَزِيزُ الْجَبَّارُ
الْمُتَكَبِّرُ ۚ سُبْحَانَ اللَّهِ عَمَّا يُشْرِكُونَ ۝ هُوَ اللَّهُ الْخَالِقُ الْبَارِئُ الْمُصَوِّرُ ۖ لَهُ
الْأَسْمَاءُ الْحُسْنَىٰ ۚ يُسَبِّحُ لَهُ مَا فِي السَّمَاوَاتِ وَالْأَرْضِ ۖ وَهُوَ الْعَزِيزُ الْحَكِيمُ

He is Allah—other than Whom there is no god, Knower of secrets and declarations. He is the Compassionate, the Merciful. He is Allah—besides Whom there is no god, the Sovereign, the Holy, the Peace-Giver, the Faith-Giver, the Overseer, the Almighty, the Omnipotent, the Majestic. Glorified is Allah, beyond what they associate. He is Allah—the Creator, the Inventor, the Designer. His are the Most Beautiful Names. Whatever is in the heavens and the Earth praises Him. And He is the Majestic, the Wise.

(*al-Ḥashr* 59:22-24)

Chapter 02

HOW DID IT ALL START?

In the previous chapter we learned that Allah ﷻ decided He was going to put a *khalifa*, a representative of Him on this Earth and that our purpose is none other than to worship Him alone. This leads to our second question: how did this Earth come into being? We know the Qur'an has the answer, as we find in *Surah al-Anbiya*, Allah ﷻ says:

أَوَلَمْ يَرَ الَّذِينَ كَفَرُوا أَنَّ السَّمَاوَاتِ وَالْأَرْضَ كَانَتَا رَتْقًا فَفَتَقْنَاهُمَا ۖ وَجَعَلْنَا مِنَ الْمَاءِ كُلَّ شَيْءٍ حَيٍّ ۖ أَفَلَا يُؤْمِنُونَ

Don't the disbelievers see that the heavens and the Earth were one entity and then we separated them and made from water every living thing. Why don't they believe?

(*al-Anbiya* 21:30)

When Allah ﷻ gives us a verse, it is not only one lesson we gain, there are many points we need to ponder upon. In this verse there are three important points.

Seeing with our heart

This verse begins with the first lesson:

أَوَلَمْ يَرَ الَّذِينَ كَفَرُوا

Those who deny the presence of Allah ﷻ, don't they see?

We can ask, what is there to see? In this ayah we are being told to see with our heart and look with our inner sight, to recognise that everything around us is a sign from Allah ﷻ to know Him, remember Him and, of course, to worship Him. Those who really want to know Allah ﷻ look at the universe which reveals many aspects of itself and then they reflect on Allah ﷻ. The first thing we need to do is to look with our heart, to think about how it all started and learn from this in order to get closer to Allah ﷻ. The next question that comes to mind then, is, how did it all start?

The separation of the heavens and the Earth

The second lesson from this verse answers this question with a scientific miracle. We are told that the heavens and the Earth are signs of Allah ﷻ,

they were initially one piece and then by Allah's ability and decision, He made them separate; the heavens went up and the Earth went down. The exact details of this are not something Allah ﷻ wanted us to know, or it would be clear in the Qur'an. What He wants us to know is proven by science now, that the heavens and Earth when joined, were made up of multiple gases which separated from each other when they became very heavy, akin to an explosion. Then they became like circles from which the Earth started and the heavens were lifted up and made into seven heavens.

Water: the source of life

The third lesson is from the last part of this verse about the human being's nature:

وَجَعَلْنَا مِنَ الْمَاءِ كُلَّ شَيْءٍ حَيٍّ

And we made from water every living thing.

أَفَلَا يُؤْمِنُونَ.

Don't they believe?'

Everything in creation, the human being and the Earth consists of 70% water, and it's the same for every living thing; almost all the animals have the same composition.

And Allah ﷻ says in another verse in *Surah al-Nur*:

:وَٱللَّهُ خَلَقَ كُلَّ دَآبَّةٍ مِّن مَّآءٍ فَمِنْهُم مَّن يَمْشِى عَلَىٰ بَطْنِهِۦ وَمِنْهُم مَّن يَمْشِى عَلَىٰ رِجْلَيْنِ وَمِنْهُم مَّن يَمْشِى عَلَىٰٓ أَرْبَعٍ يَخْلُقُ ٱللَّهُ مَا يَشَآءُ إِنَّ ٱللَّهَ عَلَىٰ كُلِّ شَىْءٍ قَدِيرٌ ۝

Allāh has created every [living] creature from water. And of them are those that move on their bellies, and of them are those that walk on two legs, and of them are those that walk on four. Allāh creates what He wills. Indeed, Allāh is over all things competent.

(al-Nur 24:45)

The Scholar Ibn Ajibah ﵀ comments that water is one of the greatest resources humans use in all its forms. From the daily need and love for it, to the lack of patience when it becomes a trial. Water is a symbol of reality, the essence of life, and humans benefit immensely from it. Created by water doesn't only mean big bodies of water, it includes other fluids too, such as semen, which the human being is created from.

Abu Hurayrah ﵁ said: 'O Messenger of Allah ﷺ, when I see you I feel happy and content, tell me about everything.' He ﷺ said: 'Everything was created from water.' I said, 'tell me about something which, if I do it, I will enter Paradise'. He ﷺ said: 'Spread (the greeting of) *Salaam*, feed others, uphold the ties of kinship, and stand in prayer at night when people are sleeping. Then you will enter Paradise in peace.' (Ahmad)

The question at the end of verse 30 in *Surah al-Anbiyah*: 'Don't they believe?' is the main message to you and I from Allah ﷻ. For fourteen centuries this question has drawn the attention of unbelievers to the great marvels God has placed in the universe, wondering how they could deny what they see everywhere. How could they persist in their disbelief when everything around them in this universe inevitably leads to faith in God, the Creator, the Wise, who conducts all affairs.

We can ask ourselves why we need to know these answers from the Qur'an, and the primary reason is that we need to translate the lessons from this into our daily life. When we see with our heart and notice the signs and the miracles of the creation all around us, then it will affect us and bring change in us.

Secondly, Allah's ﷻ ability to create and change things, is beyond the ability or understanding of any human being. One of the best ways to increase our *iman* and draw closer to Allah ﷻ is to reflect on His creation. May Allah ﷻ give us the *basira*, the insight, to look around us and to learn from all the magnificent signs He has put on this Earth. Amīn.

Points to reflect on:

- Thinking about the creation of Allah ﷻ is part of our faith and increases our *Iman*. It reminds us of how Allah ﷻ is *Al – Qawiyy* – The Strong, capable of everything.
- Contemplating about the creation of the heavens and the Earth is something that Allah ﷻ is inviting us to do. We can do this act of

worship by appreciating the smallest to the grandest details in our natural surroundings.

- Contemplation about Allah's ﷻ creation can include *dhikr* of Allah ﷻ, connecting reflection to *ibadah*.
- When we contemplate on the signs of creation, it increases our feeling of awe and love for Allah ﷻ.
- Being aware of Allah's ﷻ ability as *Al- Muqtadir*-The Creator of Power, helps us rely on Him to fulfil all our needs, because everything is in His control.

تَبَارَكَ الَّذِي بِيَدِهِ الْمُلْكُ وَهُوَ عَلَىٰ كُلِّ شَيْءٍ قَدِيرٌ ۝ الَّذِي خَلَقَ الْمَوْتَ وَالْحَيَاةَ
لِيَبْلُوَكُمْ أَيُّكُمْ أَحْسَنُ عَمَلًا ۚ وَهُوَ الْعَزِيزُ الْغَفُورُ ۝ الَّذِي خَلَقَ سَبْعَ سَمَاوَاتٍ
طِبَاقًا ۖ مَا تَرَىٰ فِي خَلْقِ الرَّحْمَٰنِ مِن تَفَاوُتٍ ۖ فَارْجِعِ الْبَصَرَ هَلْ تَرَىٰ مِن فُطُورٍ
۝ ثُمَّ ارْجِعِ الْبَصَرَ كَرَّتَيْنِ يَنقَلِبْ إِلَيْكَ الْبَصَرُ خَاسِئًا وَهُوَ حَسِيرٌ

Exalted is He in whose hand lies sovereignty, and He has power over all things. He who created death and life—to test you—which of you is best in conduct. He is the Almighty, the Forgiving. He who created seven heavens in layers. You see no discrepancy in the creation of the Compassionate. Look again. Can you see any cracks? Then look again, and again, and your sight will return to you dazzled and exhausted.

(*al-Mulk* 67:1-4)

Chapter 03

HOW DID WE COME INTO EXISTENCE?

In our journey of universal questions, we have covered why we are here and how this Earth come into existence? The natural question which follows after that is, how did *we* come to existence? Does the Qur'an shed light on how human beings came to be? Allah ﷻ answers this in two places in the Qur'an.

In the first place, Allah ﷻ informs us in *Surah al-Hajj*:

يَا أَيُّهَا النَّاسُ إِن كُنتُمْ فِي رَيْبٍ مِّنَ الْبَعْثِ فَإِنَّا خَلَقْنَاكُم مِّن تُرَابٍ ثُمَّ مِن نُّطْفَةٍ ثُمَّ
مِنْ عَلَقَةٍ ثُمَّ مِن مُّضْغَةٍ مُّخَلَّقَةٍ وَغَيْرِ مُخَلَّقَةٍ لِّنُبَيِّنَ لَكُمْ ۚ وَنُقِرُّ فِي الْأَرْحَامِ مَا
نَشَاءُ إِلَىٰ أَجَلٍ مُّسَمًّى ثُمَّ نُخْرِجُكُمْ طِفْلًا ثُمَّ لِتَبْلُغُوا أَشُدَّكُمْ ۖ وَمِنكُم مَّن يُتَوَفَّىٰ
وَمِنكُم مَّن يُرَدُّ إِلَىٰ أَرْذَلِ الْعُمُرِ لِكَيْلَا يَعْلَمَ مِن بَعْدِ عِلْمٍ شَيْئًا ۚ وَتَرَى الْأَرْضَ
هَامِدَةً فَإِذَا أَنزَلْنَا عَلَيْهَا الْمَاءَ اهْتَزَّتْ وَرَبَتْ وَأَنبَتَتْ مِن كُلِّ زَوْجٍ بَهِيجٍ

O people! If you are in doubt about the Resurrection: We created you from dust, then from a drop, then from a clinging clot, then from a lump of flesh—developed and undeveloped, to clarify things for you. And We settle in the wombs what We will, for a designated term, and then We bring you forth as infants. Then you may reach your maturity. And among you is he who is taken in [early] death, and among you is he who is returned to the most feeble [old] age so that he knows nothing, after [once having] known so much. And you see the Earth lifeless, but when We send down water on it, it stirs and swells, and grows every delightful pair of plant.

(*al-Ḥajj* 22:5)

Human development in the womb

This verse gives us clear details of how the human being came into being. The commentary of Ibn Kathir explains these stages which started with the first human Adam ﵇ created from dust. Adam's ﵇ offspring originated from semen and then the clot *'nutfah'* which settles in the woman's womb and stays in this condition for forty days. Over the next forty days, it changes into a red clot, then by the Will of Allah ﷻ, it changes into a lump of flesh until it starts to take shape with limbs. At this point of the human's development we learn from the narration of Ibn Mas'ud who said:

"The Messenger of Allah ﷺ, who is the true and truly inspired one, told us: "Every one of you is collected in the womb of his mother for the first forty days, and then he becomes a clot for another forty days, and then a lump of flesh for another forty days. Then Allah sends an angel to write four words: he writes his provision, his deeds, his life span, and whether he will be blessed or wretched. Then he blows the soul into him." (Bukhari, Muslim)

Both the hadith and the Qur'anic verse remind us about the different lifespans of people; some return back to Allah ﷻ at a young age, others mature and become strong, after which they decline and face weakness in their old age. This is made clear in another part of the Qur'an when Allah ﷻ states:

ٱللَّهُ ٱلَّذِى خَلَقَكُم مِّن ضَعْفٍ ثُمَّ جَعَلَ مِنۢ بَعْدِ ضَعْفٍ قُوَّةً ثُمَّ جَعَلَ مِنۢ بَعْدِ قُوَّةٍ ضَعْفًا وَشَيْبَةً ۚ يَخْلُقُ مَا يَشَآءُ ۖ وَهُوَ ٱلْعَلِيمُ ٱلْقَدِيرُ ۝

"Allah is He Who created you in (a state of) weakness, then gave you strength after weakness, then after strength gave (you) weakness and grey hair. He creates what He wills. And it is He Who is the All-Knowing, the All-Powerful."

(*al-Rum* 30:54)

The essence of life

The verse from *Surah al-Hajj* ends with a metaphor to bring our attention to another phenomenon:

وَ تَرَى الْأَرْضَ هَامِدَةً

And you see the Earth lifeless and still'

(*al-Hajj* 22:5)

Allah ﷻ wants us to visualise the Earth absolutely dead and lifeless and then think about what happens when He sends down rain upon it, اهْتَزَّتْ وَ رَبَتْ It begins to stir to life and swell, producing every type of pleasant plant. In this way the subject of how human life came into existence is connected to the world of plants. A parallel is made, using the word '*hamidah*' meaning the Earth is 'dry and barren', in between life and death, until rain falls on it and brings it to life with vegetation. This transformation, recorded in the Qur'an long before scientific understanding, reflects the movement of soil absorbing water and coming revitalised. The imagery also highlights the unity and shared essence of life across all living beings—plants, animals, and humans—each a sign of Allah's ﷻ Will that creates life.

Ibn Kathir's explanation reminds us that Allah's ﷻ power to bring the dead barren Earth back to life is mirrored in how He will bring the dead back to life in the hereafter. Allah ﷻ mentions our connection to the Earth in another place, *Surah Ta-Ha*:

مِنْهَا خَلَقْنَاكُمْ وَفِيهَا نُعِيدُكُمْ وَمِنْهَا نُخْرِجُكُمْ تَارَةً أُخْرَىٰ

From it, We created you. And into it, We will return you. And from it, We will bring you out another time.

(*Ta-Ha* 20:55)

Adam: The first human being created

How we came into being is answered in another *surah* of the Qur'an which connects our origin to our forefather *Sayyidina Adam* ﷺ. In this verse, Allah ﷻ states:

إِنَّ مَثَلَ عِيسَىٰ عِندَ ٱللَّهِ كَمَثَلِ ءَادَمَ ۖ خَلَقَهُۥ مِن تُرَابٍ ثُمَّ قَالَ لَهُۥ كُن فَيَكُونُ

The example of Jesus with Allah is like Adam: He created him from dust, then He said to him, 'Be! And he was.

(*Surah al-Imran* 3:59)

Here, we learn the creation of *Isa* ﷺ and Adam ﷺ from dust is a sign of Allah's ﷻ power, as when He commands something to come into existence, it does. Hawwa ﷺ was then created from Adam's rib. Prophet Muhammad ﷺ, taught us that Hawwa ﷺ was created from the rib of Adam ﷺ when he was sleeping. When Adam ﷺ woke up, he found her, and he was very happy.

Companionship is something innate in us human beings and it is natural to want to live in company with others. The name human being, *insan* is from the root word *'uns'* which means intimacy and closeness. We feel solace and happiness with a human being and chapter 6 will go into further details from the Qur'an on this subject. We now have the answer that all of mankind came from Adam and Hawwa, ﷺ.

Al-Khaliq, the Creator revealed further details in the following two verses from *Surah al-Mu'minun*:

وَ لَقَدْ خَلَقْنَا الْإِنْسَانَ مِنْ سُلٰلَةٍ مِّنْ طِيْنٍ۔ ثُمَّ جَعَلْنٰهُ نُطْفَةً فِى قَرَارٍ مَّكِيْنٍ۔ ثُمَّ خَلَقْنَا النُّطْفَةَ عَلَقَةً فَخَلَقْنَا الْعَلَقَةَ مُضْغَةً فَخَلَقْنَا الْمُضْغَةَ عِظٰمًا فَكَسَوْنَا الْعِظٰمَ لَحْمًا-ثُمَّ اَنْشَاْنٰهُ خَلْقًا اٰخَرَ-فَتَبٰرَكَ اللّٰهُ اَحْسَنُ الْخٰلِقِيْنَ

We created the human being from an extract of clay. Then We made him a drop, in a secure repository. Then We developed the drop into a clinging clot. Then We developed the clot into a lump. Then We developed the lump into bones. Then We clothed the bones with flesh. Then We produced it into another creature. Most Blessed is Allah, the Best of Creators!

(*al-Mu'minūn*, 23:12-14)

In this verse the precise stages between the human being's development are clearly outlined. Through the intimate relationship of a man and a woman, millions of sperm enter the woman, and only one enters the egg. When they meet, it becomes a *notfa*. The human being is created from a fluid that gushes forth and comes out from a place in the back where originally the testes were created. Then, in seven days it moves through the fallopian tube of the woman and reaches the uterus, where it finds a place in the uterus and clings to the wall. This is referred to as *alaqa*, a dark empty place. Then, the blood changes into flesh and at this stage, the flesh resembles a piece of chewed up chewing gum, with some indents visible. This is exactly the way Allah ﷻ describes the development, all in less than eight weeks.

The next stage of development, known as the *mudgha* continues for a very short time, after which Allah ﷻ creates bones, which are then covered by muscles. By week eight, the embryo is formed. In the translation of the verse, the word 'then' is commonly used, but the more accurate meaning implies that some time passes before the next stage of development occurs, which is now a fetus. From this point until the end of the pregnancy, the baby continues to grow in size and develops the senses of hearing and sight.

Iman and humility

What is the purpose of knowing all this, what does this remind us of? Scientific miracles make our faith stronger, but we shouldn't depend on the scientific miracles to prove that the Qur'an is true. The Qur'an is the word of Allah ﷻ, so we are not relying on a scientist to validate the Qur'an's truth. However, when we read the Qur'an, and then visually see the process of the creation of a human being, especially when we see the pictures and how Allah ﷻ describes it, our curiosity is satisfied. What else do we need as explanations from Allah ﷻ to keep our *iman* strong after all these details already exist in the Qur'an?

What we learn from this, is a very important message from Allah ﷻ. We humans tend to become arrogant and believe we are better than others. This comes about in different ways, may it be our culture or traditions etc. However, all we need to remember is, where we started from:

خَلَقْنَاكُم مِّن تُرَابٍ

We are originally from dust.
(*al-Hajj* 22:5)

مِنْهَا خَلَقْنَاكُمْ وَفِيهَا نُعِيدُكُمْ وَمِنْهَا نُخْرِجُكُمْ تَارَةً أُخْرَىٰ

From it we created you. And into it, We will return you. And from it We will bring you back out another time.
(*Ta-Ha* 20:55)

Points to reflect on:

- Contemplating on the miraculous signs within our human form leads to gratitude and awe of Allah's ﷻ mastery.
- Knowledge of the miracle of life should strengthen our relationship with Allah ﷻ.
- When we reflect on our creation and humble origin, this should remove any feeling of superiority or arrogance.
- The human being is created as a social being in need of companionship. Investing in our relationships and giving company to someone lonely are worthy deeds we can aim to do.
- Keeping our life cycle in mind, that we come from the dust of the Earth and will return back to it, should encourage us to be focused on the hereafter, our permanent home.

وَٱلتِّينِ وَٱلزَّيْتُونِ ۝ وَطُورِ سِينِينَ ۝ وَهَٰذَا ٱلْبَلَدِ ٱلْأَمِينِ ۝ لَقَدْ خَلَقْنَا
ٱلْإِنسَٰنَ فِىٓ أَحْسَنِ تَقْوِيمٍ ۝ ثُمَّ رَدَدْنَٰهُ أَسْفَلَ سَٰفِلِينَ ۝ إِلَّا ٱلَّذِينَ ءَامَنُوا۟
وَعَمِلُوا۟ ٱلصَّٰلِحَٰتِ فَلَهُمْ أَجْرٌ غَيْرُ مَمْنُونٍ ۝ فَمَا يُكَذِّبُكَ بَعْدُ بِٱلدِّينِ ۝
أَلَيْسَ ٱللَّهُ بِأَحْكَمِ ٱلْحَٰكِمِينَ ۝

By the Fig, By the olive, by Mount Sinai, by this safe town,, We created man in the finest state, then reduce him to the lowest of the low, except those who believe and do good deeds – they will have an unfailing reward. After this, what make you deny the Judgement, Is God not the most decisive of Judges?"

(*al-Tin* 95: 1-8)

Chapter 04

WHY DID WE LEAVE JANNAH?

In this chapter, we address a common question that many of us ask: Why didn't *Sayyidina* Adam ﷺ remain in Jannah, and why was he sent down to Earth? The answer is in the Qur'an and as we shall see, it teaches us great wisdom. To begin with, these verses from *Surah al-Baqarah* set the scene in Jannah where Allah ﷻ addresses our parents:

وَقُلْنَا يَا آدَمُ اسْكُنْ أَنتَ وَزَوْجُكَ الْجَنَّةَ وَكُلَا مِنْهَا رَغَدًا حَيْثُ شِئْتُمَا وَلَا تَقْرَبَا هَٰذِهِ الشَّجَرَةَ فَتَكُونَا مِنَ الظَّالِمِينَ

And We said: O Adam, stay temporarily, you and your wife in Jannah. Eat from Jannah anywhere you want, enjoy. But don't get close to this tree, otherwise you will become from the wrongdoers.
(*al-Baqarah* 2:35)

Here, we encounter the guidelines given to Adam and Hawwa ﷺ in Jannah: a temporary place to stay, with complete freedom to live at their pleasure, expressed in the word *raghadan*. The only prohibition they were told is not to approach a specific tree. Shaytan then entered this scene and lured them towards this prohibited tree which caused them to leave the gardens of Jannah.

فَأَزَلَّهُمَا الشَّيْطَانُ عَنْهَا فَأَخْرَجَهُمَا مِمَّا كَانَا فِيهِ ۖ وَقُلْنَا اهْبِطُوا بَعْضُكُمْ لِبَعْضٍ عَدُوٌّ ۖ وَلَكُمْ فِي الْأَرْضِ مُسْتَقَرٌّ وَمَتَاعٌ إِلَىٰ حِينٍ

But Satan caused them to slip from it, and he caused them to depart the state they were in. We said, 'Go down, some of you enemies to one another. And on Earth, you will have a residence and enjoyment for a while.'

(*al-Baqarah* 2:36)

Then Adam ﷺ asked for repentance and Allah ﷻ accepted his repentance as the following verse tells us:

فَتَلَقَّىٰ آدَمُ مِن رَّبِّهِ كَلِمَاتٍ فَتَابَ عَلَيْهِ ۚ إِنَّهُ هُوَ التَّوَّابُ الرَّحِيمُ

Then Adam received words from his Lord, so He accepted his repentance. He is the Acceptor of Repentance, the Merciful.

(*al-Baqarah* 2:37)

Allah ﷻ taught Adam ﷺ how to repent for his mistake, and these words of repentance are revealed in *Sūrah al-Aʿrāf*:

قَالَا رَبَّنَا ظَلَمْنَا أَنْفُسَنَا وَإِنْ لَمْ تَغْفِرْ لَنَا وَتَرْحَمْنَا لَنَكُونَنَّ مِنَ الْخَاسِرِينَ

They said, "Our Lord, we have sinned against ourselves. Unless You forgive us and have mercy on us, we will be of the losers."
(*al-Aʿrāf* 7:23)

From these *ayaat* we see the answer to the question, 'Why did they leave Jannah?'. It's because they disobeyed Allah ﷻ. However now we need to examine and understand what this teaches us. Why did Allah ﷻ put this story in the Qur'an, and what can we learn from it?

When Allah prohibits

The first thing we learn is when Allah ﷻ gives us an order, there is *hikmah*-or wisdom behind it. Generally, as human beings we don't like any kind of prohibition. We might think to ourselves, as in this case, it's just a tree, why did Allah ﷻ tell them not to eat from it? Allah ﷻ is teaching us that we have will power and choice, and we need to apply this in the way that pleases Allah ﷻ. Otherwise, if we become weak and follow every desire regardless of whether it pleases Allah ﷻ or not, there will be no difference between us and the other creatures Allah ﷻ created without wisdom or free will.

How *Shaytan* works

The second important lesson for us to learn is how *Shaytan* operates. At the point when *Shaytan* approached *Sayyidina* Adam and *Hawwa* ﷺ, they were living in Jannah as a temporary place of stay, as Allah ﷻ told them *uskun*, indicating a temporary stay. Jannah will be permanent inshaAllah, later for us, after we believe and obey Allah ﷻ by controlling our desires. The way *Shaytan* allured *Sayyidina* Adam and Hawwa was indirect, he didn't tell them 'Don't eat from the tree or you will leave Jannah', or 'Don't eat because you will be disobeying Allah ﷻ.' On the contrary he tricked them to disobey Allah ﷻ as we are told in this verse, in *Surah al-Aʿrāf*.

فَوَسْوَسَ لَهُمَا الشَّيْطَانُ لِيُبْدِيَ لَهُمَا مَا وُورِيَ عَنْهُمَا مِن سَوْآتِهِمَا وَقَالَ مَا
نَهَاكُمَا رَبُّكُمَا عَنْ هَٰذِهِ الشَّجَرَةِ إِلَّا أَن تَكُونَا مَلَكَيْنِ أَوْ تَكُونَا مِنَ الْخَالِدِينَ

But Satan whispered to them, to expose to them their nakedness, which was invisible to them. He said, "Your Lord only prohibited you from this tree so that you do not become angels or become immortals."
(*al-Aʿrāf* 7:20)

In other words, *Shaytan* suggested that Allah ﷻ didn't want them to eat from the tree because if they did, they would stay forever in Jannah. He was telling them, if you want to stay forever in Jannah eat from the tree.

This is the way *Shaytan* operates on you and I too. He beautifies the disobedience of Allah ﷻ in a way that makes us feel like we are obeying Allah ﷻ. This is a crucial message of this story for us in our daily lives. When *Shaytan* whispers,(7:20) فَوَسْوَسَ لَهُمَا الشَّيْطَانُ, and he whispers all the time, he beautifies the disobedience to Allah ﷻ in a way that makes one think 'I'm just obeying Allah', so we need to be careful.

Repentance and hope

The third, most beautiful, point here is although *Sayyidina* Adam and *Hawa* ﷺ disobeyed Allah ﷻ, Allah ﷻ accepted their repentance, which gives us hope. We should never despair from the mercy of Allah ﷻ. The moment we disobey Allah ﷻ, we acknowledge our mistake, we turn to Him, and ask for forgiveness فَتَابَ عَلَيْهِ, immediately. Allah ﷻ taught Adam ﷺ how to repent for his slip, which we found in *Surah al-A'rāf*:

قَالَا رَبَّنَا ظَلَمْنَآ أَنفُسَنَا وَإِن لَّمْ تَغْفِرْ لَنَا وَتَرْحَمْنَا لَنَكُونَنَّ مِنَ ٱلْخَـٰسِرِينَ

They said, "Our Lord, we have wronged ourselves, and if You do not forgive us and have mercy upon us, we will surely be among the losers."

(*al-A'rāf* 7:23)

Allah ﷻ didn't reprimand them and say, 'Well, I told you…', instead we are shown *Ar Rahman's* response:

فَتَلَقَّىٰ آدَمُ مِنْ رَبِّهِ كَلِمَاتٍ فَتَابَ عَلَيْهِ ۚ إِنَّهُ هُوَ التَّوَّابُ الرَّحِيمُ

Then Adam received from his Lord [some] words, and He accepted his repentance. Indeed, it is He who is the Accepting of Repentance, the Merciful.

(*al-Baqarah* 2:37)

If we want repentance, Allah is *At-Tawwāb*, the One who continually accepts the repentance of His slaves, and He is *Ar-Raheem*, the One who bestows His infinite mercy on His sinful, repentant slaves. This should give us a lot of hope.

The Prophet ﷺ also said: "If you were not to sin then Allah ﷻ would have replaced you with a people who would. Then they would seek forgiveness and would be forgiven by Allah ﷻ, because He loves to forgive. Allah ﷻ loves repentance and He loves those who repent." Being sinful is part of our humanity, and being merciful and forgiving is part of Allah's ﷻ attributes.

The message to us is not to despair. There is a reason why Allah ﷻ chose for Adam and *Hawwa* ﷺ to live for a short period in Jannah. And there is a reason why He taught you and I in many places in the Qur'an about how *Shaytan* tricks us human beings. In later chapters we will find guidance from Allah ﷻ on how to deal with a whole variety of testing situations and emotions. We must never lose hope but use our will power to fiercely resist what *Shaytan* whispers to us. If we fail, and every now and then we will surely fail, we mustn't despair. May Allah ﷻ make it easy for us to reach Jannah, our permanent home. Amīn.

Points to reflect on:

- When we are tested with trials, we can take lessons from *Sayyidina* Adam's ﷺ experience of being placed in Jannah, as part of his preparation to be *Khalifa* on Earth. What are we learning from our tests?

- Iblees and the *shayaateen* will constantly work to lure us to disobey Allah and this is a battle that will continue until the end of time on this Earth. Are we aware of our weak points that make us vulnerable?

- Through His infinite mercy, Allah ﷻ taught us how to repent and He loves us even more when we repent and turn back to Him.

- Our ultimate entrance into Jannah will come after passing tests of faith that challenge us to control our *nafs* and stay firm against the whispering of *shaytan.*

- Our goal is Jannah, the permanent residence for us inshaAllah. To reach it we have to stay humble, grateful and steadfast in our *Iman*.

قُلْ يَـٰعِبَادِىَ ٱلَّذِينَ أَسْرَفُواْ عَلَىٰٓ أَنفُسِهِمْ لَا تَقْنَطُواْ مِن رَّحْمَةِ ٱللَّهِۚ إِنَّ ٱللَّهَ يَغْفِرُ
ٱلذُّنُوبَ جَمِيعًاۚ إِنَّهُۥ هُوَ ٱلْغَفُورُ ٱلرَّحِيمُ ۝ وَأَنِيبُوا إِلَى رَبِّكُمْ وَأَسْلِمُوا لَهُ مِنْ
قَبْلِ أَنْ يَأْتِيَكُمُ الْعَذَابُ ثُمَّ لَا تُنْصَرُونَ ۝ وَاتَّبِعُوا أَحْسَنَ مَا أُنْزِلَ إِلَيْكُمْ مِنْ
رَبِّكُمْ مِنْ قَبْلِ أَنْ يَأْتِيَكُمُ الْعَذَابُ بَغْتَةً وَأَنْتُمْ لَا تَشْعُرُونَ

Say, "O My servants who have transgressed against their souls: do not despair of Allah's mercy, for Allah forgives all sins. He is the Forgiving, the Merciful." And turn to your Lord in repentance, and submit to Him, before the punishment comes upon you, and you will not be helped. And follow the best of what was revealed to you from your Lord, before the punishment comes upon you suddenly, while you are unaware."

(*Az-Zumar* 39:53-55)

Chapter 05

IS LOVE IN THE QUR'AN?

There is a bond between families and communities, between a husband and wife, between a mother and child that connects people together; this is the bond of love. Some of these ties of love are natural, for example between a parent and child, and some of these will develop during our life, as we meet people. You may wonder if the subject of love is in the Qur'an, and the answer is yes. Allah ﷻ taught us through His book that love exists on different levels and in this and the next chapter we will explore these. Our first focus is the love for Allah ﷻ. Next, there is the love for *Rasul Allah* ﷺ and then, there is of course, love between people.

Love for Allah

Do I love Allah? This is the question each one of us needs to ask ourselves. It's a significant question because we can't merely claim to love Allah ﷻ, it has to affect us. In the Qur'an we are told that if we love Allah ﷻ, it will show through our actions. What are these actions? This verse in *Surah al-Imran* makes it clear when *Rasul Allah* ﷺ is instructed to inform us:

قُلْ إِن كُنتُمْ تُحِبُّونَ اللَّهَ فَاتَّبِعُونِي يُحْبِبْكُمُ اللَّهُ وَيَغْفِرْ لَكُمْ
ذُنُوبَكُمْ ۗ وَاللَّهُ غَفُورٌ رَّحِيمٌ

Say, "If you love Allah, then follow me, and Allah will love you, and will forgive you your sins." Allah is Forgiving and Merciful
(*Āl-'Imrān* 3:31)

Hasan Al -Basri and other scholars commented that some people claimed they love Allah ﷻ, so Allah ﷻ tested them with this ayah. The meaning of this is very clear; if you follow the example of *Rasul Allah* ﷺ, Allah ﷻ will love you, وَيَغْفِرْ لَكُمْ ذُنُوبَكُمْ ۗ وَٱللَّهُ غَفُورٌ رَّحِيمٌ, and forgive your sins, as He is All-Forgiving, Most Merciful. Allah ﷻ, wants to see the *Sunnah* through our actions in how we live. This leads us to question ourselves about how we look at the *Sunnah. Do I look at the Sunnah just as something optional? For example, when I finish the obligatory prayer, do I move away and leave the sunnah prayer? Do I try to follow Rasul Allah's* ﷺ *example purely because he did it, without arguments and debates?* As many of us say, actions speak louder than words. Following the *Sunnah* is a way of showing Allah ﷻ that our feelings are sincere and a way to gain the love of Allah ﷻ. When Allah *Al – Wadud* – The Loving, loves us, there is little else we could want.

How do we know we love Allah ﷻ? One of the signs that we love Allah ﷻ is that we obey Him. This is expressed in a famous poem written by a woman, which sheds light on this. She writes:

إنْ اسْتَغصى الِهَ وَتُظْهِرُ حُبَّهُ ذَالِکَ مُحَال فِی القِيَاسِ بِدِيْعِ لَوْ کُنْتَ صَادِقًا فِی حُبِّکَ الْإطَاعک اِنَّ الْمُحِبُّ لِمَنْ يُّحِبّ الْمُطِيْع.

You disobey Allah and you claim you love Him.
This is impossible to understand.
If you were truthful in your love for Allah, you will obey Him.
Truly, the person who is in love, obeys the Beloved.

The path to gaining the love of Allah ﷻ is found in following the phrase إِنَّ اللَّهَ يُحِبُّ. 'Surely Allah loves' mentioned in the Qur'an. Each time we come across this phrase it is followed by something we can put into action. For example, Allah ﷻ loves *al-Muhsinin* ٱلْمُحْسِنِينَ *(al-Baqarah 2:195)*, those who act with excellence; *al-Muttaqin* ٱلْمُتَّقِينَ, those who are Allah conscious (*al-Tawbah* 9:4); *as-Sabireen* those who are patient and steadfast (*al-Imran* 3:146) and *al- Muqqasitin* those who act justly (*al-Maidah* 5:42). Opposite exists too; Allah ﷻ does not love those who act with injustice. Nor does He favour those who don't believe in Him or those who are ungrateful. The love of our Creator is the primary love addressed in the Qur'an.

Do I love *Rasul Allah* ﷺ ?

As we mentioned earlier, Allah ﷻ connects love for Him with following and loving the Prophet Muhammad ﷺ. This love is based on following his excellent character and actions, as Allah ﷻ says:

لَقَدْ كَانَ لَكُمْ فِي رَسُولِ اللَّهِ أُسْوَةٌ حَسَنَةٌ

Indeed, in the example of Rasul ﷺ is the best example for you' (al-Ahzab 33:21), and 'The Prophet is closer to the believers than their own selves'.

(*al-Ahzab* 33:6)

Ibn Kathir (may Allah have mercy on him) said:

"[Allah] knew how compassionate His Messenger ﷺ was towards his *Ummah*, and how sincere he was towards them, so He made him closer to them than their own selves, and decreed that his judgement among them should take precedence over their own preferences." (Tafsir Ibn Kathir, 6/380)

In response to the many false accusations the disbelievers made about *Rasul Allah* ﷺ, Allah ﷻ corrects and reminds all mankind:

وَإِنَّكَ لَعَلَىٰ خُلُقٍ عَظِيمٍ ۝

Truly you have a strong character

(*al-Qalam* 68:4)

The beautiful sublime character of the *Rasul Allah* ﷺ was captured by Aisha ﵂ in the following narration:

Sa`d bin Hisham asked A'ishah ﵂ about the character of the Messenger of Allah ﷺ, so she replied: `Have you not read the Qur'an?' Sa`d said: `Of course.' Then she said: "Verily, the character of the Messenger of Allah ﷺ was the Qur'an."' (Muslim Sahih)

In *Surah Tawba*, Allah ﷻ conveys the feelings of *Rasul Allah* ﷺ for his *ummah*, thus showing believers how deeply concerned he ﷺ was for us:

لَقَدْ جَآءَكُمْ رَسُولٌ مِّنْ أَنفُسِكُمْ عَزِيزٌ عَلَيْهِ مَا عَنِتُّمْ حَرِيصٌ
عَلَيْكُم بِٱلْمُؤْمِنِينَ رَءُوفٌ رَّحِيمٌ

A noble Messenger has come to you from among yourselves.
He's grieved by your hardships and cares about your wellbeing,
for the believers he is compassionate and kind.

(*al-Tawba* 9:128).

How can we increase in our love for *Rasul Allah* ﷺ? By learning more about his noble characteristics and step by step, incorporating his way – his *sunnah* – into our lives consistently, we will be demonstrating our love for him. Believers are also encouraged to say *salawat* as often as possible, as we are told:

مَا مِنْ أَحَدٍ يُسَلِّمُ عَلَيَّ إِلَّا رَدَّ اللَّهُ عَلَيَّ رُوحِي حَتَّى أَرُدَّ عَلَيْهِ السَّلَامَ

"None of you who send me their salutation (salam), except that Allah returns my soul and I return him his greeting."

(Sunan Abi Daud)

The love between relatives and friends

Is love between people covered in the Qur'an? Yes, the legendary love of *Sayyidina* Yaqub ﷺ for his son, *Sayyidina* Yusuf ﷺ is an example. This father's ﷺ affection was well known which caused his other sons to say:

إِذْ قَالُوا لَيُوسُفُ وَأَخُوهُ أَحَبُّ إِلَىٰ أَبِينَا.

'Recall when they said: 'Surely Yusuf and his brother are more beloved to our father'

(*Yusuf* 12:8)

Sayyidina Yaqub ﷺ continued grieving Yusuf's ﷺ absence, crying for years until he became blind because he missed him. This is the natural love of a father for a son, and is one of several familial bonds of love covered in the Qur'an.

Allah ﷻ is our Creator and He knows us, therefore He cautions us about love between people in *Surah al-Baqarah*

وَمِنَ النَّاسِ مَنْ يَتَّخِذُ مِنْ دُونِ اللَّهِ أَنْدَادًا يُحِبُّونَهُمْ كَحُبِّ اللَّهِ ۖ وَالَّذِينَ آمَنُوا أَشَدُّ حُبًّا لِلَّهِ ۗ

Yet among the people are those who take others as Allah's equals. They love them (more) than the love for Allah. But those who believe have a greater love for Allah.

(*al-Baqarah* 2:165)

This verse compares two groups of people. The first are those who follow their feelings and their love for people goes over and above Allah's ﷻ commands. They are willing to disobey Allah ﷻ, because of the people they love and make equal to Him.

Then Allah ﷻ says وَالَّذِينَ آمَنُوا the true believer أَشَدُّ حُبًّا لِلَّه loves Allah ﷻ more than anything else. To love Allah ﷻ more than anything else is a daily struggle we all go through. Often we have to make a decision about doing something we might love, but we know Allah ﷻ doesn't love it. At this point, we need to ask ourselves 'Where does my love for Allah ﷻ stand?' The opposite is also true; if we follow something in obedience to Allah ﷻ, and do something He loves, that we don't really want to do, or like doing, then again, we can ask ourselves 'Where do I place my love for

Allah ﷻ,is this a priority in my life?' If we can overcome our *nafs* and act in obedience, then this is proof of our love. There is a beautiful verse from *Surah al Kahf* – The Cave, which guides us to keep the company of those who please Allah ﷻ, in preference to those who seek only the pleasures of this world.

وَٱصْبِرْ نَفْسَكَ مَعَ ٱلَّذِينَ يَدْعُونَ رَبَّهُم بِٱلْغَدَوٰةِ وَٱلْعَشِىِّ يُرِيدُونَ وَجْهَهُۥ ۖ وَلَا تَعْدُ
عَيْنَاكَ عَنْهُمْ تُرِيدُ زِينَةَ ٱلْحَيَوٰةِ ٱلدُّنْيَا ۖ وَلَا تُطِعْ مَنْ أَغْفَلْنَا قَلْبَهُۥ
عَن ذِكْرِنَا وَٱتَّبَعَ هَوَىٰهُ وَكَانَ أَمْرُهُۥ فُرُطًا ۝

Content yourself with those who pray to their Lord morning and evening, seeking His approval, and do not let your eyes turn away from them out of desire for the attractions of this worldly life: do not yield to those whose hearts We have made heedless of Our Qur'an, those who follow their own low desires, those whose ways are unbridled.

(*al-Kahf* 18:28)

May Allah ﷻ spread love on this Earth to all his creations and between all his creations, but most importantly, that His ﷻ love becomes number one in every one of us. Amīn.

Points to reflect on:

- Are our actions aligned to the love we feel for Allah ﷻ? Reflecting on our daily routines and how to include the sunnah will help us.
- If we want to feel the love of Allah ﷻ, we need to develop those qualities we find in the Qur'an which He loves: patience, justice, steadfastness, repentance and reliance upon Him, amongst other qualities.
- The more we learn about the conduct of *Rasul Allah* ﷺ, the more our love for him will increase insha Allah.
- We can take account of ourselves by checking how the people in our lives influence us, including our immediate family. The more we love someone, the more we conform to their wishes. Is Allah ﷻ and what He wants from us the top priority in our life?
- Love between friends starts with the company we choose. This can take us closer to obeying Allah ﷻ and *Rasul Allah* ﷺ or further away. Each of us is responsible for this.

لَّيْسَ ٱلْبِرَّ أَن تُوَلُّوا۟ وُجُوهَكُمْ قِبَلَ ٱلْمَشْرِقِ وَٱلْمَغْرِبِ وَلَٰكِنَّ ٱلْبِرَّ مَنْ ءَامَنَ بِٱللَّهِ
وَٱلْيَوْمِ ٱلْءَاخِرِ وَٱلْمَلَٰٓئِكَةِ وَٱلْكِتَٰبِ وَٱلنَّبِيِّۦنَ وَءَاتَى ٱلْمَالَ عَلَىٰ حُبِّهِۦ ذَوِى ٱلْقُرْبَىٰ
وَٱلْيَتَٰمَىٰ وَٱلْمَسَٰكِينَ وَٱبْنَ ٱلسَّبِيلِ وَٱلسَّآئِلِينَ وَفِى ٱلرِّقَابِ وَأَقَامَ ٱلصَّلَوٰةَ
وَءَاتَى ٱلزَّكَوٰةَ وَٱلْمُوفُونَ بِعَهْدِهِمْ إِذَا عَٰهَدُوا۟ ۖ وَٱلصَّٰبِرِينَ فِى ٱلْبَأْسَآءِ وَٱلضَّرَّآءِ
وَحِينَ ٱلْبَأْسِ ۗ أُو۟لَٰٓئِكَ ٱلَّذِينَ صَدَقُوا۟ ۖ وَأُو۟لَٰٓئِكَ هُمُ ٱلْمُتَّقُونَ ۝

Righteousness does not consist in turning your face towards East or West. The truly good are those who believe in God and the Last Day, in the angels, the Scripture, and the prophets; who give away some of their wealth, however much they cherish it, to their relatives, to orphans, the needy, travelers and beggars, and to liberate those in bondage; those who keep up the prayer and pay the prescribed alms; who keep pledges whenever they make them; who are steadfast in misfortune, adversity, and times of danger. These are the ones who are true, and it is they who are aware of God.

(*al-Baqarah* 2:177)

Chapter 06

IS MARRIAGE IN THE QUR'AN?

In the previous chapter, we covered how love for Allah ﷻ and His Messenger ﷺ is explored in the Qur'an. In this chapter, we find answers to another common question about the natural feelings Allah ﷻ puts inside us, one of which is the love between the opposite genders. Adam ﷺ was lonely in Jannah and Allah ﷻ created *Hawwa* ﷺ from his rib. The need for companionship is absolutely natural and something Allah ﷻ approves of. However, He also taught us how to channel these feelings through marriage. So, we find marriage and the love between a married couple *is* in the Qur'an.

Affection and Mercy

One of the most common verses that is recited during a wedding ceremony, is this verse from *Surah al-Rum*,

وَمِنْ آيَاتِهِ أَنْ خَلَقَ لَكُم مِّنْ أَنفُسِكُمْ أَزْوَاجًا لِّتَسْكُنُوا إِلَيْهَا وَجَعَلَ بَيْنَكُم مَّوَدَّةً وَرَحْمَةً ۚ إِنَّ فِي ذَٰلِكَ لَآيَاتٍ لِّقَوْمٍ يَتَفَكَّرُونَ

And of His signs is that He created for you from yourselves mates that you may find tranquility in them; and He placed between you affection and mercy. Indeed in that are signs for a people who give thought.

(*al-Rum* 30:21)

Through the generations since Adam and *Hawwa* ﷺ, marriage is the only channel to translate the feelings between a man and a woman. Allah ﷻ describes feelings between the married couple using a beautiful word: '*mawadda*', not love '*hubb*'. He said, وَجَعَلَ بَيْنَكُم مَّوَدَّةً وَرَحْمَةً He has placed 'affection and mercy' between the spouses. *Mawadda* is affection and friendship; it also means intimacy, mercy, and taking care of each other. The richness of this Arabic word includes trusting each other and sacrifice for each other, all in this one word.

In addition, Allah ﷻ used the word وَرَحْمَةً *rahma*, in which this context means loving, mercy, grace and empathy. We all know things don't always go smoothly in married life. Feelings of love evolve with time into *mawadda*. But sometimes the *mawadda* may decrease because a problem occurs between the couple. Then there is a need for *rahma*. When a spouse has mercy, even if the love weakens temporarily, they will treat their *zawj* -spouse with compassion, forgiveness and patience, in short in a way that pleases Allah ﷻ. So when things don't go well and feelings change, we need to pause a little and remember the goal of married life and the attitude we should have.

It's remarkable how Allah ﷻ constructs the verse and chooses His words. He ends the verse by telling us the creation of *azwaj*- spouses, is a sign and He ends the verse with 'إِنَّ فِى ذَٰلِكَ لَءَايَٰتٍ' – '*Indeed in that are signs*'. Allah ﷻ is telling us that in marriage are signs for those who reflect and think.

Marriage is highly recommended

Marriage in Islam is highly recommended. Naturally, *Rasul Allah* ﷺ addressed young people specifically and said, يا مَعْشَرَ شباب youth, men and women, عليكم بِالبَاء, get married. فَمَنْ لَمْ يَسْتَطِعْ If they can't afford it, فليصم, then he recommended fasting.

> 'Abdallah ibn Mas'ud reported God's Messenger ﷺ as saying, "Young man, those of you who can support a wife should marry, for it keeps you from looking at strange women and preserves you from immorality; but those who cannot, should devote themselves to fasting, for it is a means of suppressing sexual desire."
>
> * (Bukhari and Muslim)

Why did he ﷺ say this? He said this because fasting will help protect ones chastity. In Islam, chastity and morality are extremely important in the Muslim community, and the only way to channel the natural feelings He put in us, is through marriage.

The Messenger of Allah ﷺ said: "There are three, whom it is a right upon Allah ﷻ to help: one who gets married seeking chastity; a slave who makes a contract with his master with the aim of buying his freedom; and one who fights for the sake of Allah ﷻ." (Ahmad)

In this hadith we learn that amongst the three people Allah ﷻ will help is the young person who wants to get married for chastity but he cannot, meaning he can't afford it. A person in this situation has a right upon Allah ﷻ to help them.

Marriage came as an order in the Qur'an in *Surah al-Nur*-the chapter of Light:

وَأَنكِحُوا الْأَيَامَىٰ مِنكُمْ وَالصَّالِحِينَ مِنْ عِبَادِكُمْ وَإِمَائِكُمْ ۚ إِن يَكُونُوا فُقَرَاءَ
يُغْنِهِمُ اللَّهُ مِن فَضْلِهِ ۗ وَاللَّهُ وَاسِعٌ عَلِيمٌ

And wed those who are single among you. And those who are righteous among your servants and maids. If they are poor, Allah will enrich them from His bounty. Allah is All-Encompassing, All-Knowing.

(*al-Nūr* 24:32)

Here Allah ﷻ tells us to get married to righteous people. Again, He knows that some can't afford it and He consoles those who are poor that He will provide for them. Richness does not only mean Allah ﷻ will give us physical money or objects, it can mean making us feel content and satisfied.

Muslims need to look at marriage as the nucleus of our community. Marriage is not only about feelings and companionship, but there is a responsibility that comes with it. There is sacrifice, patience and the natural feeling of love which will translate into the feelings that Allah ﷻ wants from us in our marriages: friendship; taking care of each other; compassion.

May Allah ﷻ bless every marriage and make it easy for everyone. May Allah ﷻ put understanding between every couple that is going through difficulties. Amīn.

Points to reflect on:

- The Qur'an highlights the natural need for companionship and established marriage for the benefit of the individual and the family unit which protects both spouses.
- Marriage needs to be approached with a purpose: a means to preserve chastity; an act of *ibadah* as we are obeying Allah ﷻ and following the *Sunnah*, and a means by which to get closer to Him.
- Seeing our spouse as a mercy and gift from Allah ﷻ will help to grow mutual respect. Compassion and love are also a gift from Allah ﷻ and something we should be grateful for.
- Marriage is our contribution to a bigger cause: helping society in preserving morality, and protecting family values and virtues.

- Married life will have tests, just like other areas of our life. With *taqwa* – God consciousness, patience and forgiveness couples can overcome the everyday issues with ease.

- When there are conflicting messages in society about marriage and married life, we have the clear guidance about marriage from Allah ﷻ Who sets specific rights and responsibilities for spouses too.

رَبَّنَا هَبْ لَنَا مِنْ أَزْوَاجِنَا وَذُرِّيَاتِنَا قُرَّةَ أَعْيُنٍ وَاجْعَلْنَا لِلْمُتَّقِينَ إِمَامًا

"Our Lord, grant us from among our spouses and offspring comfort to our eyes and make us an example for the righteous."

(*al-Furqan* 25:74)

Chapter 07

DOES THE QUR'AN DISCUSS PREGNANCY?

One of the purposes of marriage is to have a family as we explored in the previous chapter. The next logical question that comes to mind is about the part of life we see around us regularly, which is pregnancy. Is this subject mentioned in the Qur'an? Yes, the development of a new life is in the Qur'an, which has not left anything out which is important for us to know. Sometimes a subject is mentioned in great detail and other times it is covered briefly. In *Surah al-A'rāf*, Allah ﷻ gives precise details:

هُوَ الَّذِي خَلَقَكُم مِّن نَّفْسٍ وَاحِدَةٍ وَجَعَلَ مِنْهَا زَوْجَهَا لِيَسْكُنَ إِلَيْهَا ۖ فَلَمَّا تَغَشَّاهَا حَمَلَتْ حَمْلًا خَفِيفًا فَمَرَّتْ بِهِ ۖ فَلَمَّا أَثْقَلَت دَّعَوَا اللَّهَ رَبَّهُمَا لَئِنْ آتَيْتَنَا صَالِحًا لَّنَكُونَنَّ مِنَ الشَّاكِرِينَ ۝ فَلَمَّا آتَاهُمَا صَالِحًا جَعَلَا لَهُ شُرَكَاءَ فِيمَا آتَاهُمَا ۚ فَتَعَالَى اللَّهُ عَمَّا يُشْرِكُونَ ۝

It is He who created you from a single being, and He made its mate from it, so that he may find comfort in her. Then, when he has covered her, she conceives a light load, and she carries it around. But when she has grown heavy, they pray to Allah their Lord, "If You give us a good child, we will be of the thankful." But when He has given them a good child, they attribute partners to Him in what He has given them. Exalted is Allah above what they associate.

(*al-A'rāf* 7:189-190)

What do we learn from here? Allah ﷻ is giving the context to pregnancy here when He says He created mates to live in security, safety and happiness together. First of all, we learn the Qur'an does not leave topics out; this is a book where the intimate relationship, فَلَمَّا تَغَشَّاهَا between a husband and wife is mentioned. Allah ﷻ used a very eloquent word تَغَشَّاهَا– *taghshaha* – 'he covers her', to tell us that this is not only a physical need being fulfilled, but it is also a spiritual and emotional need – it is comprehensive.

The Stages of Pregnancy

The Qur'an describes the stages of pregnancy as فَلَمَّا تَغَشَّاهَا حَمَلَتْ حَمْلًا خَفِيفًا in which حَمْلًا خَفِيفًا at first is very light, meaning the first four to eight weeks. The woman sometimes doesn't even know she is pregnant yet. After this is the next stage فَلَمَّا أَثْقَلَت , from twenty weeks the woman starts feeling the pregnancy more. From twenty eight weeks or seven months onwards, she's heavier and by nine months the pregnancy is very heavy. At this stage there are more challenges, like sleeping becomes difficult and for some women even breathing becomes difficult.

Being thankful for a child

The above *ayah* describes how parents at this point turned to Allah ﷻ and they said, لَئِنْ آتَيْتَنَا صَالِحًا . They made a covenant with Allah ﷻ, making dua together 'Ya Allah, if you give us a righteous, healthy girl or boy – whatever it is they wanted-we will be grateful'. Allah ﷻ responded and gave them what they wanted. Then He says, 'you made a partner with Me.'

What could this 'partner' mean? Allah ﷻ gave the couple a child and if the child became more important than their Creator, and the reason why they disobey Allah ﷻ, then this makes the child equal to Allah ﷻ. This can happen at any stage, when parents want to please their child – young or adult, and they cross the limits set by Allah ﷻ for their son or daughter's sake. This is not gratefulness. Gratefulness, on the contrary, is simply using what Allah ﷻ gave us in a way that pleases Him. He gave you what you begged Him for. Righteous, healthy child. Or you prayed for a specific gender and He fulfilled this too. We are being warned not to make the child the reason for gaining Allah's ﷻ displeasure.

At the end of the verse, He says, فَتَعَالَى اللَّهُ عَمَّا يُشْرِكُونَ. Allah ﷻ is exalted. Even if someone tries to make anything equal to Allah ﷻ, He is above anything that is taken as a partner.

What Allah ﷻ is telling us here through something as natural as pregnancy is a reminder to us that it is Allah ﷻ Who made it happen.

Allah's ﷻ knowledge about the unborn child

In another verse in the Qur'an, we are told:

اللَّهُ يَعْلَمُ مَا تَحْمِلُ كُلُّ أُنثَىٰ وَمَا تَغِيضُ الْأَرْحَامُ وَمَا تَزْدَادُ

Allah knows what every female carries, and what increases and decreases in the wombs.

(*al-Ra'd* 13:8)

Allah ﷻ knows every uterus. It is difficult to imagine that He is aware of what every uterus of a woman carries وَمَا تَغِيضُ الْأَرْحَامُ وَمَا تَزْدَادُ. He alone knows if the pregnancy will be lost or if it will be multiple with twins or triplets.

The Qur'an has everything we need. The words Allah ﷻ uses in the Qur'an, teaches us in great depth. The intimate relationship is described in many ways; as a cover and as love for spiritual and emotional needs. The most important lesson for us is everything Allah ﷻ gives us is a blessing and we need to use this blessing in the way that pleases Him. Otherwise, Allah ﷻ is not in need of our gratitude or anything from us. May Allah ﷻ make us among the grateful. Amīn.

Points to reflect on:

- Our relationship with our spouses brings us *sakeenah* that we need to use to get closer to Allah ﷻ.
- We were created with a need to become parents at one point in our lives. Pregnancy is natural and Allah ﷻ created this honour and blessing in a woman, thus we should not be afraid of it.
- We should make *du'a* to Allah ﷻ to give us a '*Saalih*' child who will be pleasing to Allah ﷻ. Both parents should be making *du'a*, as both parents raise the child, not only one of them.
- Allah ﷻ is *al- Khaliq*, He creates and He only knows if and when a woman will carry a baby. Remembering this should humble us.
- We need to be careful with not putting our child above Allah ﷻ in our priorities.
- We should be constantly aware that Allah ﷻ is the source of our happiness, and everything we have is from Him. Just as He has given a blessing to us, He can remove it. Thus, we need to be grateful.

يَـٰٓأَيُّهَا ٱلنَّاسُ إِنَّا خَلَقْنَـٰكُم مِّن ذَكَرٍ وَأُنثَىٰ وَجَعَلْنَـٰكُمْ شُعُوبًا وَقَبَآئِلَ لِتَعَارَفُوٓا۟ ۚ إِنَّ
أَكْرَمَكُمْ عِندَ ٱللَّهِ أَتْقَىٰكُمْ ۚ إِنَّ ٱللَّهَ عَلِيمٌ خَبِيرٌ

"O mankind, indeed We have created you from male and female and made you nations and tribes that you may know one another. Indeed, the most noble of you in the sight of Allāh is the most righteous of you. Indeed, Allāh is Knowing and Aware."

(*al-Hujurat* 49:13)

Chapter 08

IS CHILDBIRTH IN THE QUR'AN?

As the Qur'an speaks about marriage and pregnancy, this naturally leads us to another common question, especially for women, but also for men: is childbirth mentioned in the Qur'an? Indeed, yes it is. It's in the story of *Sayyidah* Maryam, in *Surah Maryam* Chapter 19. Allah says:

فَحَمَلَتْهُ فَانتَبَذَتْ بِهِ مَكَانًا قَصِيًّا ۝ فَأَجَاءَهَا الْمَخَاضُ إِلَىٰ جِذْعِ النَّخْلَةِ قَالَتْ
يَا لَيْتَنِي مِتُّ قَبْلَ هَٰذَا وَكُنتُ نَسْيًا مَّنسِيًّا

So she conceived him, and withdrew with him to a remote place. The labour-pains drove her to the trunk of the palm-tree. She said, "I wish I had died before this, and been completely forgoten."

(*Maryam* 19:22-23)

Labour pains

Sayyida Maryam's pregnancy was different and unique, as there was no man (husband) in her life. Allah ﷻ blew from His spirit and she became pregnant. What did she then do? Now pregnant, she withdrew to a remote place. When she reached full term, the reality of the pains of labour drove her to the trunk of a palm tree, which she held on to as the pains increased. And then she cried from what she was experiencing, wishing she had died before this, and been completely forgotten by people.

Experiencing a pregnancy, labour pains and delivery is something many woman will go through, and its importance is reinforced in the way Allah ﷻ mentioned it in detail in the Qur'an. He could have simply said the baby was delivered, but He went into the detail of what a woman experiences through the process of labour. The word *makhāḍ* specifically refers to contractions during labour, and not just the delivery.

Support during labour

فَنَادَاهَا مِن تَحْتِهَا أَلَّا تَحْزَنِي قَدْ جَعَلَ رَبُّكِ تَحْتَكِ سَرِيًّا ۝ وَهُزِّي إِلَيْكِ بِجِذْعِ
النَّخْلَةِ تُسَاقِطْ عَلَيْكِ رُطَبًا جَنِيًّا ۝ فَكُلِي وَاشْرَبِي وَقَرِّي عَيْنًا

Whereupon he called her from beneath her: "Do not be sad; your Lord has placed a stream beneath you. And shake towards you the trunk of the palm-tree; and fresh, ripe dates will fall upon you. So eat, and drink, and be cheerful."

(*Maryam* 19:24-26)

A reassuring voice, فَنَادَىٰهَا, which is actually *Sayyidina Isa* ﷺ, calls to her from under the tree, telling her not to grieve and worry. The comforting voice tells *Sayyida* Maryam ﷺ that her Lord has provided a stream under her feet and if she shakes the trunk of the palm, fresh ripe dates will fall. so that she can eat, drink, feel at ease and not worry.

There are two vital lessons we learn here. The first is about taking action. *Sayyidah* Maryam ﷺ was in pain, she was sad and worried. While *Sayyidah* Maryam ﷺ felt like this, this relates to other women too, who may be single for example if their husband passed away. They too would face pregnancy alone, possibly with no family around them and this is a situation which is not uncommon all over the world.

Allah ﷻ told Maryam ﷺ to shake the palm tree and 'eat, drink from the water under you, and don't worry.' Why did He ask her to shake the palm tree? Allah ﷻ could have easily sent the dates to her. The first lesson Allah ﷻ is teaching us is to take action, to use the resources we have and work for what we want.

The second is that woman in labour need support. Apart from the need for food and drink, she needs to feel good and for someone to support her. In the case of *Sayyidah* Maryam ﷺ, she was alone and experienced fear and anxiety, but Allah ﷻ was with her and *Sayyidina Isa* ﷺ was under her. When we are aware of a woman going through labour, we need to empathise with her and offer her help and support. Through the permission and blessings of Allah ﷻ, these days there are many ways to ease the labour experience, but in some parts of the world, these facilities are not available at all. *Sayyidah* Maryam ﷺ is told وَقَرِّى عَيْنًا, to 'cool her eyes' when she sees her newborn, which is the universal experience for every woman who is in delivery; the sight of the baby overtakes the labour pains a mother has just experienced.

Post delivery Social support:

The narration continues with an instruction on how to deal with people *Sayyidah* Maryam ﷺ would see:

فَإِمَّا تَرَيِنَّ مِنَ ٱلْبَشَرِ أَحَدًا فَقُولِىٓ إِنِّى نَذَرْتُ لِلرَّحْمَـٰنِ صَوْمًا فَلَنْ أُكَلِّمَ ٱلْيَوْمَ إِنسِيًّا

And if you see any human, say, "I have vowed a fast to the Most Gracious—so I will not speak to any human today."
(*Maryam* 19:26)

This verse concludes the scene of *Sayyidah* Maryam's ﷺ labour, after which her son, *Sayyidina Isa* ﷺ speaks to the people, as the miracle bestowed on this Prophet of Allah and something Allah ﷻ gave especially for *Sayyidah* Maryam ﷺ – the best of all women. He said to her when you are worried about what the people will say, don't talk, and tell them you don't want to talk. Instead, it is her blessed son ﷺ who will speak for her and relieve her situation.

In these beautiful five verses in the Qur'an, Allah ﷻ is teaching humanity that labour is painful and stressful. He helped *Sayyidah* Maryam ﷺ who was alone without a labour room, without physicians or nurses, there was no husband or support. But Allah ﷻ helped her. For any woman who is approaching labour, or has just discovered she is pregnant, the message is not to worry as Allah ﷻ will make a way and send ease.

The other message from these verses is for women to take whatever assistance is available to make things easy for themselves, alongside depending on Allah's ﷻ help.

Remembering the process of labour and childbirth leads to recalling this amazing process is a *ni'mah*-a blessing. When a life comes out of a life it is the greatest miracle of all miracles. As it says in *Surah an-Nahl*:

وَاللَّهُ أَخْرَجَكُمْ مِنْ بُطُونِ أُمَّهَاتِكُمْ لَا تَعْلَمُونَ شَيْئًا

And Allah brought you out of your mothers' wombs, not knowing anything.

(*an-Nahl* 16:78)

May Allah ﷻ make things easy for every woman going to go through labour. And may Allah ﷻ give everyone a righteous child who is a coolness to their parents eyes. Amīn.

Points to reflect on:

- Allah ﷻ focuses on the reality of labour pains with compassion to remind humankind of the great hardship a mother goes through during delivery.
- Women in childbirth need all types of support. How can we offer support to an expecting mother before, during and after labour?

- Remembering the help of Allah ﷻ is near; He helps us at times of extreme stress and hardship. He is the One we depend on.

- Whatever our situation is at childbirth, or during an illness or any other type of test, we are reminded in the story of *Sayyidah* Maryam ﷺ to take action to help ourselves.

- Educating our families about the psychological, emotional and physical needs of a mother at perinatal and postnatal stages should be a high priority in our family, social and community circles. How can we bring this change?

- Birth is a miracle by Allah's ﷻ permission. Recalling this helps those who would like to conceive but may not have yet. Everything is by Allah's ﷻ Will.

وَوَصَّيْنَا الْإِنسَانَ بِوَالِدَيْهِ إِحْسَانًا ۖ حَمَلَتْهُ أُمُّهُ كُرْهًا وَوَضَعَتْهُ كُرْهًا ۖ وَحَمْلُهُ
وَفِصَالُهُ ثَلَاثُونَ شَهْرًا ۚ حَتَّىٰ إِذَا بَلَغَ أَشُدَّهُ وَبَلَغَ أَرْبَعِينَ سَنَةً قَالَ رَبِّ أَوْزِعْنِي
أَنْ أَشْكُرَ نِعْمَتَكَ الَّتِي أَنْعَمْتَ عَلَيَّ وَعَلَىٰ وَالِدَيَّ وَأَنْ أَعْمَلَ صَالِحًا تَرْضَاهُ
وَأَصْلِحْ لِي فِي ذُرِّيَّتِي ۖ إِنِّي تُبْتُ إِلَيْكَ وَإِنِّي مِنَ الْمُسْلِمِينَ
أُولَٰئِكَ الَّذِينَ نَتَقَبَّلُ عَنْهُمْ أَحْسَنَ مَا عَمِلُوا وَنَتَجَاوَزُ عَن سَيِّئَاتِهِمْ فِي أَصْحَابِ
الْجَنَّةِ ۖ وَعْدَ الصِّدْقِ الَّذِي كَانُوا يُوعَدُونَ

We have instructed the human bring to kindness to his parents. His mother carried him with difficulty, and she delivered him with difficulty. His bearing and weaning take thirty months. Until, when he has reached his prime at the age of forty, he says, "My Lord, enable me to appreciate the blessings You have bestowed upon me and upon my parents, and to act with righteousness, pleasing You. And also make my descendants righteous. I have sincerely repented to You, and I am of those who submit." Those are from whom We accept the best of their deeds, and We overlook their misdeeds—among the inhabitants.

(*al-Ahqaf* 46:15)

Chapter 09

ARE BREASTFEEDING AND WEANING MENTIONED IN THE QUR'AN?

When a mother has delivered her baby, the first need to be fulfilled is feeding the new infant. In this chapter, we ask if the subject of breastfeeding and weaning are in the Qur'an? Yes, the subject is found in depth. In the following detailed verse, Allah ﷻ lays out many principles for both parents. In *Surah al-Baqarah* it is stated:

وَالْوَالِدَاتُ يُرْضِعْنَ أَوْلَادَهُنَّ حَوْلَيْنِ كَامِلَيْنِ ۖ لِمَنْ أَرَادَ أَنْ يُتِمَّ الرَّضَاعَةَ ۚ وَعَلَى الْمَوْلُودِ لَهُ رِزْقُهُنَّ وَكِسْوَتُهُنَّ بِالْمَعْرُوفِ ۚ لَا تُكَلَّفُ نَفْسٌ إِلَّا وُسْعَهَا

And let mothers nurse their infants for two full years, for those who desire to complete the nursing. It is the duty of the father to provide for them and clothe them in a proper manner. No soul shall be burdened beyond its capacity.

(*al-Baqarah* 2:233)

The mothers may يُرْضِعْنَ أَوْلَادَهُنَّ breastfeed their newborn for حَوْلَيْنِ كَامِلَيْنِ two years for whoever wishes to complete this duration. It doesn't have to be two years, as it's a choice. In that period, the father is responsible for the child and the mother's provision, taking care of her financially and emotionally, according to what is acceptable in that society. This is in keeping with the principle that no person is charged with more than what he or she has the capacity to do; Allah ﷻ will only ask us to do what we can manage: لَا تُكَلَّفُ نَفْسٌ إِلَّا وُسْعَهَا *No soul shall be burdened beyond its capacity*; (*al-Baqarah* 2:233). These general principles about the parents, responsibilities and the newborn's rights are for all people, but it is also important to note these verses are embedded within rules relating to divorce in this *Surah*. Allah ﷻ sets limits that ensure justice and protects the vulnerable in all situations.

Mutual agreement between parents:

ا تُضَارَّ وَالِدَةٌ بِوَلَدِهَا وَلَا مَوْلُودٌ لَهُ بِوَلَدِهِ ۚ وَعَلَى الْوَارِثِ مِثْلُ ذَٰلِكَ ۗ فَإِنْ أَرَادَا فِصَالًا عَنْ تَرَاضٍ مِنْهُمَا وَتَشَاوُرٍ فَلَا جُنَاحَ عَلَيْهِمَا ۗ وَإِنْ أَرَدْتُمْ أَنْ تَسْتَرْضِعُوا أَوْلَادَكُمْ فَلَا جُنَاحَ عَلَيْكُمْ إِذَا سَلَّمْتُمْ مَا آتَيْتُمْ بِالْمَعْرُوفِ

No mother shall be harmed on account of her child, nor shall a father be harmed on account of his child. The same duty rests upon the heir. If they desire separation, by mutual consent and consultation, they commit no error by doing so. You commit no error by hiring nursing-mothers, as long as you pay them fairly.

(*al-Baqarah* 2:233)

The next part of the verse states no mother should be harmed because of her child and no father should be harmed due to his child. If the father dies, then the father's heir must still take care of the mother and child. Then we see the mercy of Allah ﷻ in this verse. If both the father and the mother agree mutually to stop breastfeeding, there is no harm and this is also fine. The verse lays out clearly that if they decide that the mother is not going to continue to breastfeed for whatever reason, and they decide to hire someone to nurse their child, there is no blame upon them as long as they both agree and the wet nurse is paid according to what is acceptable. Then Allah ﷻ reminds us to be aware of Him, and do everything with *ihsan* – with excellence. There is responsibility on both the woman and the man to take care of each other and to be concious of Allah ﷻ. The verse ends with: وَاللَّهُ بِمَا تَعْمَلُونَ بَصِيرٌ '*He is seeing everything we are doing*'; this reminder underlines all that precedes it.

Gratitude to Allah and parents

Pregnancy and breastfeeding are also mentioned later on in the Qur'an. In *Surah al-Ahqaf*, Allah ﷻ said the following, وَوَصَّيْنَا ٱلْإِنسَـٰنَ بِوَٰلِدَيْهِ إِحْسَـٰنًا 'have enjoined the human being to treat his parents with *ihsan*, utmost excellence'. The verse then continues to shed light on pregnancy and nursing:

وَوَصَّيْنَا ٱلْإِنسَـٰنَ بِوَٰلِدَيْهِ إِحْسَـٰنًا ۖ حَمَلَتْهُ أُمُّهُۥ كُرْهًا وَوَضَعَتْهُ كُرْهًا ۖ وَحَمْلُهُۥ
وَفِصَـٰلُهُۥ ثَلَـٰثُونَ شَهْرًا ۚ حَتَّىٰٓ إِذَا بَلَغَ أَشُدَّهُۥ وَبَلَغَ أَرْبَعِينَ سَنَةً قَالَ رَبِّ أَوْزِعْنِىٓ
أَنْ أَشْكُرَ نِعْمَتَكَ ٱلَّتِىٓ أَنْعَمْتَ عَلَىَّ وَعَلَىٰ وَٰلِدَىَّ وَأَنْ أَعْمَلَ صَـٰلِحًا تَرْضَىٰهُ
وَأَصْلِحْ لِى فِى ذُرِّيَّتِىٓ ۖ إِنِّى تُبْتُ إِلَيْكَ وَإِنِّى مِنَ ٱلْمُسْلِمِينَ ۝

And We have enjoined upon man, to his parents, good treatment. His mother carried him with hardship and gave birth to him with hardship, and his gestation and weaning [period] is thirty months. [He grows] until, when he reaches maturity and reaches [the age of] forty years, he says, "My Lord, enable me[1] *to be grateful for Your favour which You have bestowed upon me and upon my parents and to work righteousness of which You will approve and make righteous for me my offspring. Indeed, I have repented to You, and indeed, I am of the Muslims."*

(*al-Ahqaf* 46:15)

This verse from *Surah al-Ahqaf*, when read with the *ayah* from *Surah al-Baqarah* we have just covered, points to a scientific miracle of the Qur'an.

Allah ﷻ calculates the pregnancy and nursing as a total of thirty months. If we subtract the twenty-four months of breastfeeding previously mentioned, then this *ayah* indicates the pregnancy could be a minimum of six months. Modern day medicine confirms that the minimum length of pregnancy for a child to survive after delivery is six months. So the Qur'an summarises this possibility in one statement of thirty months and this is considered the initial length of hardship a mother goes through.

Reaching forty years – a turning point

The verse continues with a beautiful message for us all about the cycle of life and what is expected of us as we age. What are we supposed to do when we reach the age of forty? This is the only age specifically mentioned in the Qur'an, and we are told to turn to Allah ﷻ with *du'a* for help and are reminded to be grateful for our blessings and parents. This age is not positioned in the Qur'an as a time of mid-life crisis; instead it's a time to reflect, ask for guidance and do good deeds. Before this point, a person may have been busy with studying or building a career. Now at forty, most people have settled and so this *du'a* is asking for the ability to focus on good deeds.

Finally the *du'a* extends to asking for one's children to be righteous. Maybe some parents feel they could have done better, and they turn to Allah ﷻ at this stage to ask for help with their children. These verses show the cycle of life, with the focus being on turning to Allah ﷻ and repenting to Him. When we celebrate turning forty, it should include how we turn to Allah ﷻ fully and restate our position: '*I am from the Muslims*'. We are reminded here that Islam is more than identifying with a religious label. The verse calls on us to say: *'I am now, Ya Allah, from those who will submit to your Will'*.

May Allah ﷻ put barakah and blessing in our family, in our children, in every pregnant woman, in every delivery, in every breastfeeding woman. And May Allah ﷻ bless us all to live this *du'a* and hear the response to it, and allow us to live and die in a state of Islam. Amīn.

Points to reflect on:

- Allah ﷻ guides both the mother and father to consult mutually about the baby's welfare. We can extend this principle to our parenting generally.

- The protection of the mother and baby is prioritised in this divine book and serves as a message to all who have women and children under their care.
- The Qur'an makes it clear that there is choice in relation to nursing and there should be no compulsion. When advising new mothers this principle is a good guideline.
- Reaching the age of maturity is a blessing and opportunity to reflect and improve.
- Allah ﷻ reminds us to be grateful to Him and our parents for their hardships because we are likely to forget this.

وَإِذْ قَالَ لُقْمَانُ لِابْنِهِ وَهُوَ يَعِظُهُ يَا بُنَيَّ لَا تُشْرِكْ بِاللَّهِ ۖ إِنَّ الشِّرْكَ لَظُلْمٌ عَظِيمٌ ۝ وَوَصَّيْنَا الْإِنسَانَ بِوَالِدَيْهِ حَمَلَتْهُ أُمُّهُ وَهْنًا عَلَىٰ وَهْنٍ وَفِصَالُهُ فِي عَامَيْنِ أَنِ اشْكُرْ لِي وَلِوَالِدَيْكَ إِلَيَّ الْمَصِيرُ ۝ وَإِن جَاهَدَاكَ عَلَىٰ أَن تُشْرِكَ بِي مَا لَيْسَ لَكَ بِهِ عِلْمٌ فَلَا تُطِعْهُمَا ۖ وَصَاحِبْهُمَا فِي الدُّنْيَا مَعْرُوفًا ۖ وَاتَّبِعْ سَبِيلَ مَنْ أَنَابَ إِلَيَّ ۚ ثُمَّ إِلَيَّ مَرْجِعُكُمْ فَأُنَبِّئُكُم بِمَا كُنتُمْ تَعْمَلُونَ ۝ يَا بُنَيَّ إِنَّهَا إِن تَكُ مِثْقَالَ حَبَّةٍ مِّنْ خَرْدَلٍ فَتَكُن فِي صَخْرَةٍ أَوْ فِي السَّمَاوَاتِ أَوْ فِي الْأَرْضِ يَأْتِ بِهَا اللَّهُ ۚ إِنَّ اللَّهَ لَطِيفٌ خَبِيرٌ ۝

When Luqman said to his son, as he advised him, "O my son! Do not associate any partners with Allah—idolatry is a terrible wrong." And We entrusted the human being with the care of his parents. His mother carried him through hardship upon hardship, and his weaning takes two years. So give thanks to Me, and to your parents. To Me is the destination. But if they pressure you to associate with Me what you have no knowledge of, do not obey them. But keep them company in this life, in kindness, and follow the path of him who turns to Me. Then to Me is your return, and I will inform you of what you used to do.

(*Luqmān* 31:13-15)

Chapter 10

PARENTS

What does the Qur'an say about parents?

When we think of the most common relationship on this Earth, the first thing that comes to our mind is that of a parent and child. With this universal bond, we expect this subject to be mentioned in the Qur'an, but from what angle? The subject of parents is mentioned in the Qur'an approximately ten times. In general, the verses are about how we should treat them well, with kindness and excellence.

Tawheed and honouring parents

The first time parents are mentioned is in *Surah al-Baqarah* when Allah ﷻ says:

وَإِذْ أَخَذْنَا مِيثَاقَ بَنِي إِسْرَائِيلَ لَا تَعْبُدُونَ إِلَّا اللَّهَ وَبِالْوَالِدَيْنِ إِحْسَانًا وَذِي
الْقُرْبَىٰ وَالْيَتَامَىٰ وَالْمَسَاكِينِ وَقُولُوا لِلنَّاسِ حُسْنًا وَأَقِيمُوا الصَّلَاةَ وَآتُوا الزَّكَاةَ

We made a covenant with the Children of Israel: "Worship none but Allah. And be good to parents, relatives, orphans and the needy; speak kindly to people; perform the prayer and give zakat."

(*al-Baqarah* 2:83)

Allah ﷻ is speaking here for the first time in the Qur'an about this concept, to worship none but God and to show kindness to parents and their close relatives, and then to orphans, and then to the poor. The thing that we all have to pay attention to is that Allah ﷻ put 'worship none but Allah' – *tawheed*-the active affirmation of the oneness of Allah ﷻ and with it وَبِالْوَالِدَيْنِ إِحْسَانًا kindness to parents.

Now if we move a little bit forward in the Qur'an, we're going to see in *Surah al-Nisa* – the chapter of the woman, Allah ﷻ now gives us instructions as an order.

وَٱعْبُدُوا۟ ٱللَّهَ وَلَا تُشْرِكُوا۟ بِهِۦ شَيْـًٔا ۖ وَبِٱلْوَٰلِدَيْنِ إِحْسَـٰنًا وَبِذِى ٱلْقُرْبَىٰ وَٱلْيَتَـٰمَىٰ
وَٱلْمَسَـٰكِينِ وَٱلْجَارِ ذِى ٱلْقُرْبَىٰ وَٱلْجَارِ ٱلْجُنُبِ وَٱلصَّاحِبِ بِٱلْجَنۢبِ وَٱبْنِ ٱلسَّبِيلِ
وَمَا مَلَكَتْ أَيْمَـٰنُكُمْ

'Worship Allah, and don't associate anything with Him; be kind to parents, to relatives, to orphans, to the needy, to those neighbours you know well and those you don't, to travellers and to the slaves you own.'

(*al-Nisā'* 4:36)

We are being clearly told not to associate anything with Allah ﷻ, and in the same way as the previous verse, it is paired with treating our parents with kindness. This verse goes into more details, including relatives, with emphasis on different kinds of neighbours.

In *Surah al-An'am*-the Cattle, Allah ﷻ directly addresses us; once again saying do not associate anything with Allah ﷻ, وَبِلْوَالِدَيْنِ إِحْسَانًا and this is paired with treating our parents with kindness and excellence. The verse continues with discouraging any indecency, وَلَا تَقْرَبُوا۟ ٱلْفَوَٰحِشَ مَا ظَهَرَ مِنْهَا وَمَا بَطَنَ. whether external or internal.

قُلْ تَعَالَوْا۟ أَتْلُ مَا حَرَّمَ رَبُّكُمْ عَلَيْكُمْ ۖ أَلَّا تُشْرِكُوا۟ بِهِۦ شَيْـًٔا ۖ وَبِٱلْوَٰلِدَيْنِ إِحْسَـٰنًا ۖ وَلَا تَقْتُلُوٓا۟ أَوْلَـٰدَكُم مِّنْ إِمْلَـٰقٍ ۖ نَّحْنُ نَرْزُقُكُمْ وَإِيَّاهُمْ ۖ وَلَا تَقْرَبُوا۟ ٱلْفَوَٰحِشَ مَا ظَهَرَ مِنْهَا وَمَا بَطَنَ ۖ وَلَا تَقْتُلُوا۟ ٱلنَّفْسَ ٱلَّتِى حَرَّمَ ٱللَّهُ إِلَّا بِٱلْحَقِّ ۚ ذَٰلِكُمْ وَصَّىٰكُم بِهِۦ لَعَلَّكُمْ تَعْقِلُونَ ۝

Say, 'Come! I will tell you what your Lord has really forbidden you. Do not ascribe anything as a partner to Him; be good to your parents; do not kill your children in fear of poverty' We will provide for you and for them ' stay well away from committing obscenities, whether openly or in secret; do not take the life God has made sacred, except by right. This is what He commands you to do: perhaps you will use your reason."

(*al-An'am* 6:151)

Lower the wings of humility

We turn now to a more detailed message on how to treat parents in *Surah al-Isra*, Bani Israel. It starts with the same concept as the other *ayaat*: not to worship anyone but Allahﷻ, إِيَّاهُ وَبِٱلْوَٰلِدَيْنِ إِحْسَـٰنًا and then how to treat parents with excellence.

وَقَضَىٰ رَبُّكَ أَلَّا تَعْبُدُوا إِلَّا إِيَّاهُ وَبِالْوَالِدَيْنِ إِحْسَانًا ۚ إِمَّا يَبْلُغَنَّ عِندَكَ الْكِبَرَ أَحَدُهُمَا أَوْ كِلَاهُمَا فَلَا تَقُل لَّهُمَا أُفٍّ وَلَا تَنْهَرْهُمَا وَقُل لَّهُمَا قَوْلًا كَرِيمًا

Your Lord has commanded that you worship none but Him, and to be good to your parents. If either of them, or both of them, reaches old age with you: do not say to them words of disrespect, nor scold them, but speak to them respectfully.

(*al-Isrā'* 17:23)

The second part of this verse comes with a tough message. When either of the elderly parents reach old age which is a big challenge for them and those around them, we are told not to say even '*uff*' or anything inappropriate to them. Instead, we are told to speak to them with gentleness and honour.

وَٱخْفِضْ لَهُمَا جَنَاحَ ٱلذُّلِّ مِنَ ٱلرَّحْمَةِ.

The ending of this verse is a beautiful imagery and *du'a*; lower the wings of humility to them and make *du'a* for them. ٱلرَّحْمَةِ وَقُل رَّبِّ ٱرْحَمْهُمَا كَمَا رَبَّيَانِى صَغِيرًا. The *du'a* we are being taught is saying: Ya Allah, have mercy on them in *dunya* and in *akhirah*, just the same way they loved and cared for me when I was vulnerable, and they raised me.

You may wonder what '*uff*' means? The word '*uff*' in nowadays is when we roll our eyes in the presence of our parents, when we slam the door because we don't like what they said, or they wanted something from us which is a little bit hard or at an inconvenient time and we just shrug our shoulders and walk away. Or we answer back to their requests with 'why me?'. Allah ﷻ reminds us how respecting parents can be easy, if we remember what they did for us. We can recall how they raised us when we were very young; the mother waking up at two or three in the morning, because we were crying or the father who worked so hard to help us to reach where we are now-we mustn't forget their efforts. In this vein, the companion of *Rasul Allah* ﷺ, Abu Hurayrah ؓ reported Allah's Messenger emphasising the need to serve and care for elderly parents when he ﷺ said:

"Let him be humbled, let him be humbled. It was said: Allah's Messenger ﷺ, who is he? He said: He who finds his parents in old age, either one or both of them, and does not enter Paradise" (*Muslim*)

We find, in the narrations about prophets, the same standard. *Sayyidina Yahya* ؑ is described in *Surah Maryam* as one who:

"وَبَرًّا بِوَٰلِدَيْهِ وَلَمْ يَكُن جَبَّارًا عَصِيًّا"

"And [he was] dutiful to his parents, and he was not disobedient or rebellious."
(*Maryam* 19:14)

Sayyidina Isa ؑ is another example of obedience. Immediately after he was born, he said I will treat my mother with utmost kindness, وَبَرًّا بِوَالِدَتِي in the best way:

قَالَ إِنِّى عَبْدُ ٱللَّهِ ءَاتَىٰنِىَ ٱلْكِتَـٰبَ وَجَعَلَنِى نَبِيًّا ۝
وَجَعَلَنِى مُبَارَكًا أَيْنَ مَا كُنتُ وَأَوْصَـٰنِى بِٱلصَّلَوٰةِ وَٱلزَّكَوٰةِ مَا دُمْتُ حَيًّا ۝
وَبَرًّۢا بِوَٰلِدَتِى وَلَمْ يَجْعَلْنِى جَبَّارًا شَقِيًّا ۝
وَٱلسَّلَـٰمُ عَلَىَّ يَوْمَ وُلِدتُّ وَيَوْمَ أَمُوتُ وَيَوْمَ أُبْعَثُ حَيًّا ۝

Isa spoke: 'I am a servant of Allah; He has given me the Book, made me a prophet, made me blessed wherever I go, commanded me to pray and to give charity as long as I live, and [made me] dutiful to my mother and He has not made me overbearing or disobedient. So Allah's peace be on me the day I was born, the day I will die, and the day I will be resurrected.'

(*Maryam* 19: 30-33)

Non-Muslim parents:

Allah ﷻ in *Surah Luqman* teaches us how to treat parents even if they are not Muslims.

حَمَلَتْهُ أُمُّهُ وَهْنًا عَلَىٰ وَهْنٍ وَفِصَالُهُ فِي عَامَيْنِ أَنِ اشْكُرْ لِي
وَلِوَالِدَيْكَ إِلَيَّ الْمَصِيرُ ۝

وَإِن جَاهَدَاكَ عَلَىٰ أَن تُشْرِكَ بِي مَا لَيْسَ لَكَ بِهِ عِلْمٌ فَلَا
تُطِعْهُمَا ۖ وَصَاحِبْهُمَا فِي الدُّنْيَا مَعْرُوفًا ۝

His mother carried him through hardship upon hardship, and his weaning takes two years. So give thanks to Me, and to your parents. To Me is the destination. But if they pressure you to associate with Me what you have no knowledge of, do not obey them. But keep them company in this life, in kindness.

(*Luqmān* 31: 14-15)

Within this verse that enjoins gratitude to parents and is a reminder about the mother's hardships, we are also told not to obey them if they have enjoined others with God, or have pushed us to do things that are displeasing to Allah ﷻ. Here, and this is the only time that we're told not to obey them, we are *still* reminded to عِلْمٌ فَلَا تُطِعْهُمَا ۖ وَصَاحِبْهُمَا فِى ٱلدُّنْيَا مَعْرُوفًا, be with them, treat them well and treat them with kindness. But we're not supposed to follow them in any way that is not pleasing to Allah ﷻ.

As we explored in the previous chapter, the fact that the mother went through pregnancy, childbirth and nursing is the basis for the respect she deserves.

So, for us, what we need to learn here is, treating parents well is one of the most important values in Islam, after *Iman* and the five pillars. Indeed the excellent treatment of parents is associated with worshipping and obeying Allah ﷻ alone. Even if things become difficult, in terms of the relationship with parents, we still have to stay focused on Jannah and where we want to be. We need to bear in mind what pleases Allah ﷻ and also remember how our parents went through so many difficulties when we were young and they took care of us.

Why does the Qur'an emphasise the treatment of parents?

One more question that comes to mind is: why did Allah ﷻ put so much emphasis on children treating their parents well but there is less said about parents caring for their children? This is fascinating because parents treating children well is a natural instinct.

Usually, it is natural for parents to take very good care of their children, and so we don't find several reminders about this in the Qur'an. Sometimes, parents can even go way above and beyond necessities to please their children. In the Sunnah of *Rasul Allah* ﷺ we find a balanced approach in many of his sayings about compassion, mercy and fairness toward our children. He ﷺ said 'He who does not show mercy (towards children), no mercy would be shown to him' (Sahih Muslim) and 'Your children have the right to receiving equal treatment, as you have the right that they should honour you.' (Abu Dawud).

When the children grow into adults, and their parents grow old, that's where the challenge of worldliness – the *dunya* and its distractions in our own lives can lead to us neglecting our parents, and they could become less important. The roles reverse, as we grow older, we have less need of them, and when they grow older, their need for our support increases. In contemporary society, things have changed completely, but we shouldn't change as Muslims because our *deen's* values don't change. Treating parents well comes straight after worshipping Allah ﷻ alone. If we ask any Muslim, '*do you worship Allah ﷻ only?*' the answer is '*yes*'. When any one of us asks ourselves, '*do I treat my parents well?*', the answer should also be absolutely, '*yes!*' May Allah ﷻ bless all our parents, help us to be aware of our responsibility and to practise care for our elderly parents. Ya Rabbi Amīn.

Points to reflect on:

- Knowing that obedience to parents is obedience to Allah ﷻ will help us to be patient with them and invest in building our relationship with them.
- We need to humble ourselves before our parents and do our best not to hurt them, avoid shouting at them, doing things behind their back, or anything that may dishonour them.
- Even when we don't like something about them, or if we see them doing which is not pleasing to Allah ﷻ, we need to choose our words wisely, and be as kind as possible in our communication with them.
- If we live away from home, then calling them, visiting them regularly, doing good deeds in their name and making *du'a* for them should be a part of our regular *'ibaadah* routine.
- We can never be grateful enough or repay our parents for all the good they have done for us, but we can serve them to the best of our ability.
- Sometimes it is not easy to be kind to our parents. Many parents have abused their children and did awful, violent things to them. We need to be aware that we cannot control our feelings, however, what we can control is our words and deeds. We should still be kind to them with the intention that our behaviour towards them is to please Allah ﷻ alone.

رَبَّنَا اغْفِرْ لِي وَلِوَالِدَيَّ وَلِلْمُؤْمِنِينَ يَوْمَ يَقُومُ الْحِسَابُ

Our Lord! Forgive me, my parents, and the believers on the Day when the judgment will come to pass.

(*Ibrahim* 14:41)

Chapter 11

CHILDREN

What does the Qur'an say about children?

In previous chapters we delved into what the Qur'an says about our purpose, how Allah ﷻ brought us into existence and our closest relationships. Now the question about children comes to mind; what does the Qur'an say about children? As we will see, the subject is covered in the Qur'an in many ways, giving us a balanced view. We'll start with the primary message which is that children are amongst the blessings Allah ﷻ gives us in this world.

Children as a blessing

وَاللَّهُ جَعَلَ لَكُم مِّنْ أَنفُسِكُمْ أَزْوَاجًا وَجَعَلَ لَكُم مِّنْ أَزْوَاجِكُم بَنِينَ وَحَفَدَةً
وَرَزَقَكُم مِّنَ الطَّيِّبَاتِ ۚ أَفَبِالْبَاطِلِ يُؤْمِنُونَ وَبِنِعْمَتِ اللَّهِ هُمْ يَكْفُرُونَ

And Allah made for you spouses from yourselves.
And He produced for you, from your spouses, children, and grandchildren.
And He provided you with good things. Will they believe in falsehood and show ingratitude for Allah's blessings?

(*an-Nahl* 16:72)

This verse establishes that children are a *ni'mah* – a blessing. We have to remember this regardless of even if they are challenging or develop in ways we find difficult. If we experience hardship or distress because of them, then deal with them patiently, we will be rewarded for this.

The second message Allah ﷻ reminds us of is that this *dunya* – world, is beautiful and there are two main components in the beauty of this world which we find, as listed in *Surah al-Kahf*:

الْمَالُ وَالْبَنُونَ زِينَةُ الْحَيَاةِ الدُّنْيَا ۖ وَالْبَاقِيَاتُ
الصَّالِحَاتُ خَيْرٌ عِندَ رَبِّكَ ثَوَابًا وَخَيْرٌ أَمَلًا

Wealth and children are the decorations of the present life.
But the things that last, the virtuous deeds, are better with your Lord for reward, and better for hope.

(*al-Kahf* 18:46)

What is Allah ﷻ telling us here? He is affirming that children are part of the beauty of this world and that it's good to have them. In other parts of the Qur'an, they are described as a source of joy too.

Praying for a child

There are accounts in the Qur'an of prophets who asked Allah ﷻ for children and when Allah ﷻ granted their *du'a*-prayers, they were delighted. *Sayyidina Ibrahim's* ﷺ specific *du'a* is an example:

رَبِّ هَبْ لِي مِنَ الصَّالِحِينَ

My Lord, grant me one of the righteous [offspring].

(*al-Saffat* 37:100)

And in relation to this *du'a*, in *Surah Hud*, we learn *Sayyidinna Ibrahim's* wife Sarah ﷺ laughed at the good news of being blessed with a child. Even though she was surprised, exclaiming 'I am going to have a child, and I'm very old', she was pleased about the fact that Allah ﷻ was going to bless her.

وَامْرَأَتُهُ قَائِمَةٌ فَضَحِكَتْ فَبَشَّرْنَاهَا بِإِسْحَاقَ وَمِنْ وَرَاءِ إِسْحَاقَ يَعْقُوبَ

And his wife was standing by, so she laughed.
Then We gave her good news of Isaac; and after Isaac, Jacob.

(*Hud* 11:71)

The Prophet *Sayyidina Zakariya* ﷺ asked Allah ﷻ to give him a child so that he is not left without an heir to inherit from him. Allah ﷻ revealed:

وَزَكَرِيَّآ إِذْ نَادَىٰ رَبَّهُۥ رَبِّ لَا تَذَرْنِى فَرْدًا وَأَنتَ خَيْرُ ٱلْوَٰرِثِينَ ۞
فَٱسْتَجَبْنَا لَهُۥ وَوَهَبْنَا لَهُۥ يَحْيَىٰ وَأَصْلَحْنَا لَهُۥ زَوْجَهُۥٓ إِنَّهُمْ كَانُوا۟ يُسَٰرِعُونَ فِى
ٱلْخَيْرَٰتِ وَيَدْعُونَنَا رَغَبًا وَرَهَبًا ۖ وَكَانُوا۟ لَنَا خَٰشِعِينَ ۞

'Remember Zakariya, when he cried out to his Lord, "My Lord, do not leave me childless, although You are the Best of Inheritors. We answered him – We gave him Yahya and cured his wife of barrenness – they were always keen to do good deeds. They called upon Us out of longing and awe, and humbled themselves to Us."

(*al-Anbiya* 21:89-90)

The Qur'ān teaches us to pray specifically for righteous offspring:

وَالَّذِينَ يَقُولُونَ رَبَّنَا هَبْ لَنَا مِنْ أَزْوَاجِنَا وَذُرِّيَّاتِنَا قُرَّةَ أَعْيُنٍ وَاجْعَلْنَا لِلْمُتَّقِينَ إِمَامًا

And those who say, "Our Lord! Grant us that our spouses and our offspring be a joy to our eyes, and do make us the leaders of the God-fearing."

(*al-Furqān* 25:74)

So, asking Allah ﷻ for children is absolutely recommended. He's the only One Who gives permission for us to have a child, even the *Anbiya* needed to have this blessing. Making *du'a* so that Allah ﷻ gives us righteous children is therefore found through these prophet's accounts. Allah ﷻ said this in *Surah al-Furqan* when he was describing *Ibadur Rahman*, the real servants of *Rahman*.

Sayyidina Ibrahim ﷺ made a *du'a* for a child: رَبِّ هَبْ لِى مِنَ ٱلصَّـٰلِحِينَ, So we should make *du'a* not only for children but to be given a righteous child: 'Ya Allah, grant me a righteous child' is a good *du'a* to make in keeping with the Qur'an.

Children as a test for us

Having established children are a blessing, Allah ﷻ warns us they can also be a test. Many people will identify with this. Allah ﷻ says in *Surah al-Anfal*:

وَاعْلَمُوا أَنَّمَا أَمْوَالُكُمْ وَأَوْلَادُكُمْ فِتْنَةٌ وَأَنَّ اللَّهَ عِنْدَهُ أَجْرٌ عَظِيمٌ

And know that your possessions and your children are a test, and that with Allah is an immense reward.

(*al-Anfāl* 8:28)

Here we are told our wealth, money and our children are trials for us. Why is that? How can something we all ask Allah ﷻ for, something we want as the coolness of our eyes, which we love so much, be a trial? Children become a trial if they become a distraction from Allah ﷻ. It could also be the unfortunate case where parents, for the sake of pleasing their children, might disobey Allah ﷻ. Then they become a reason of disobedience and sometimes in extreme cases, of abandoning the values of Islam completely.

The basic issue here is not to let any human being, even if they are the closest to us or the answer to our *du'a*, take us away from Allah ﷻ, which is why we are reminded in the Qur'an:

يَا أَيُّهَا الَّذِينَ آمَنُوا لَا تُلْهِكُمْ أَمْوَالُكُمْ وَلَا أَوْلَادُكُمْ عَن ذِكْرِ اللَّهِ ۚ وَمَن يَفْعَلْ ذَٰلِكَ فَأُولَٰئِكَ هُمُ الْخَاسِرُونَ

O Believer, do not let your wealth and children distract you from the remembrance of Allah. And whosoever does that, they are absolute losers.

(*al-Munafiqun* 63:9)

The following verse from the Qur'an which according to scholars, was revealed in relation to a Companion who had children whom he loved very much. Every time he wanted to go on an expedition with *Rasul Allah* ﷺ, they used to stand in front of him and start crying and his heart softened. He didn't want to leave them and go with *Rasul Allah* ﷺ, after which this verse was revealed:

يَا أَيُّهَا الَّذِينَ آمَنُوا إِنَّ مِنْ أَزْوَاجِكُمْ وَأَوْلَادِكُمْ عَدُوًّا لَّكُمْ فَاحْذَرُوهُمْ

O you who believe! Among your spouses and your children are enemies to you, so beware of them.
(*al-Taghābun* 64:14)

Allah ﷻ addresses us all here, 'O believers', this is you and I. In this verse we are being made aware of the possibility of being misled by family. As we read the Qur'an, one thing we have to remember is the verses apply to us here and now, as they did at the time of revelation.

When we read the Qur'an, the first question we need to ask ourselves: 'Is this verse describing me? Is my child taking me away from Allah ﷻ?' It is difficult to ask ourselves this because children are very dear to us, yet we have to be honest with ourselves. If we find there is a problem, we need to turn to Allah ﷻ and ask Him to make it easy, and for our children *not* be an obstacle between us and Him.

Ideally, the converse should be our goal: we should help our children come closer to Allah ﷻ. In reality, some of us will be tested just as the prophets of Allah ﷻ were tested. *Sayyidina Nuh* ﷺ was tested with his son. He had two sons, one was a firm believer and obedient to his father and the second one was not, and died as a *kafir*- disbeliever. So we see they can be a test, a challenge and in rare cases, even an enemy. Having said that, children generally, are a blessing from Allah ﷻ and they are the 'coolness of the eyes' and most of the time they can be a reason to bring us closer to Allah ﷻ.

May Allah ﷻ make every child a coolness to their parents' eyes, and also make them a reason for continuous charity – *sadaqa jariyah*-for their parents after they pass away. Amīn.

Points to reflect on:

- Children are a blessing we should be grateful for.
- Making *du'a* for righteous children is recommended as the Prophets of Allah ﷻ did.
- Remembering that our children are part of the beauty and enjoyment of this worldly life encourages patience with them.
- Allah ﷻ reminds us that children can be a test and trial if they cause their parents to disobey Allah ﷻ. We need to assess our actions and be aware of who we prioritise: Allah ﷻ is our first priority.
- When we find ourselves challenged by our children, we need to remember these times are opportunities for our spiritual growth and Allah's ﷻ reward, so long as we are patient and just.
- Raising our children with a strong connection to the *deen* is their right. Righteous children who pray for their parents are a source of *sadaqah jariyah* – continuous charity – after parents pass away.

قُلْ إِنَّ رَبِّى يَبْسُطُ ٱلرِّزْقَ لِمَن يَشَآءُ وَيَقْدِرُ وَلَـٰكِنَّ أَكْثَرَ ٱلنَّاسِ لَا يَعْلَمُونَ ۝
وَمَآ أَمْوَٰلُكُمْ وَلَآ أَوْلَـٰدُكُم بِٱلَّتِى تُقَرِّبُكُمْ عِندَنَا زُلْفَىٰٓ إِلَّا مَنْ ءَامَنَ وَعَمِلَ صَـٰلِحًا
فَأُو۟لَـٰٓئِكَ لَهُمْ جَزَآءُ ٱلضِّعْفِ بِمَا عَمِلُوا۟ وَهُمْ فِى ٱلْغُرُفَـٰتِ ءَامِنُونَ ۝ وَٱلَّذِينَ
يَسْعَوْنَ فِىٓ ءَايَـٰتِنَا مُعَـٰجِزِينَ أُو۟لَـٰٓئِكَ فِى ٱلْعَذَابِ مُحْضَرُونَ ۝

Say [Prophet], 'My Lord gives in abundance to whoever He wills and sparingly to whoever He wills, though most people do not understand. Neither wealth nor children will bring you nearer to Us, but those who believe and do good deeds will have multiple rewards for what they have done, and will live safely in the lofty dwellings of Paradise whereas those who work against Our messages, seeking to undermine them, will be summoned to punishment.'

(*Saba* 34:36-38)

Chapter 12

IS COMMUNITY MENTIONED IN THE QUR'AN?

Wherever we live in the world, be that in a large town or small village, we are all part of the *Ummah* – the global community of Muslims. Does the Qur'an say anything about this community? Yes, in the Qur'an Allah ﷻ described Muslims as the best people. Before we discover why, Allah ﷻ instructed us with an order to:

وَاعْتَصِمُوا بِحَبْلِ اللَّهِ جَمِيعًا وَلَا تَفَرَّقُوا ۚ وَاذْكُرُوا نِعْمَتَ اللَّهِ عَلَيْكُمْ إِذْ كُنتُمْ أَعْدَاءً فَأَلَّفَ بَيْنَ قُلُوبِكُمْ فَأَصْبَحْتُم بِنِعْمَتِهِ إِخْوَانًا وَكُنتُمْ عَلَىٰ شَفَا حُفْرَةٍ مِّنَ النَّارِ فَأَنقَذَكُم مِّنْهَا ۗ كَذَٰلِكَ يُبَيِّنُ اللَّهُ لَكُمْ آيَاتِهِ لَعَلَّكُمْ تَهْتَدُونَ

And hold firmly to the rope of Allah, all together, and be not divided. And remember Allah's favour upon you; when you were enemies, and He united your hearts, and by His grace you became brothers. And you were on the pit of fire and He saved you from it. Thus Allah makes clear to you his verse that you will be guided.

(*al-Imrān* 3:103)

The Rope of Allah ﷻ

What is the 'rope of Allah' that we are told as a community, and the *ummah* of Muhammad ﷺ, to hold onto? The two widely accepted commentaries on this interpret this rope as the Qur'an itself and the community. So we need to hold firmly onto the book of Allah ﷻ. *Rasul Allah* ﷺ said in a hadith in Ibn Majah, as *Imam* Tabari explained in his commentary:

كتابَ اللهِ ممدودٌ ما بينَ السَّماءِ والأرضِ

The book of Allah is the rope that is between the heavens and the Earth

Holding onto the Qur'an, learning the Qur'an, practising the Qur'an, understanding the Qur'an and struggling to understand the Qur'an will bring us all together. It is the one thing we all share; we have the same book, the same Qur'an-the rope of Allah ﷻ. So, وَاعْتَصِمُوا بِحَبْلِ اللهِ جَمِيعًا, as an *ummah* and as a nation, we should avoid what divides us. We need to look at what brings us together, instead of focusing on what separates us.

The qualities that please Allah ﷻ

Our *Rasul* ﷺ said in a beautiful hadith which teaches you and I about this: 'إِنَّ اللهَ يَرْضَى لَكُمْ ثَلَاثًا وَيَسْخَطُ لَكُمْ ثَلَاثًا Allah is pleased when you have three qualities and He is unhappy, displeased when you have three.' What are these? The hadith continues: 'He likes أن تعبدوه، ولا تشركوا به شيئا. that we worship Him and do not associate anyone with him.' The second thing is the same concept: وأن تعتصموا بحبل الله جميعا. " Hold onto the rope of Allah" – which implies holding onto the community and to the Qur'an. وأن تناصحوا من ولاه الله أمركم ' and you advise your leaders.'

ويسخط لكم What are the three things He doesn't like? They are one: 'vain talk '.قِيلَ وَقَالَ , such as discussing what others said وإضاعة المال. The second is wasting wealth. وَكَثْرَةُ السُّؤَالِ The third is asking too many unnecessary questions.

As part of an *ummah*, these three things to do, and three to avoid, are a part of holding on to the rope of Allah ﷻ. Allah ﷻ then commends our *ummah* further on in *Surah Al-'Imran*:

كُنتُمْ خَيْرَ أُمَّةٍ أُخْرِجَتْ لِلنَّاسِ تَأْمُرُونَ بِٱلْمَعْرُوفِ وَتَنْهَوْنَ عَنِ ٱلْمُنكَرِ وَتُؤْمِنُونَ بِٱللَّهِ ۗ وَلَوْ ءَامَنَ أَهْلُ ٱلْكِتَـٰبِ لَكَانَ خَيْرًا لَّهُم ۚ مِّنْهُمُ ٱلْمُؤْمِنُونَ وَأَكْثَرُهُمُ ٱلْفَـٰسِقُونَ

'You are the best community that ever emerged for humanity: you advocate what is moral, and forbid what is immoral, and believe in Allah. . If only the People of the Scripture had believed, it would have been better for them. Among them are believers, but most of them are defiantly disobedient.

(*al-'Imrān* 3:110)

Start with myself

We have to be reflective and ask ourselves 'why has Allah ﷻ said this? Is it because we are simply Muslims? ' No, the truth is, much more is required of us.

تأمرون بالمعروف وتنهون عن المنكرWe should enjoin good and prevent evil. This means we should advise people to do good and encourage people to stay away from the disobedience of Allah ﷻ and the *al-munkar*, those rejected things that Allah ﷻ is not pleased with. Our role involves three things; belief in only Allah ﷻ, enjoining what is good and pleases Him, and preventing evil – or all those things He does not want us to do.

To do this, we can start with our souls first, and train ourselves to keep away from what displeases Allah ﷻ. Only then can we start teaching people. Being a Muslim is not enough, it's what we do in this life and the good we can encourage that matters. *Imam* ibn Majah reported that the Messenger of Allah ﷺ said, انتُم تُوفُّونَ سَبعِينَ أمّةً أنتُم خَيرُها وَأكرَمُها عَلَى الله. 'You are the final of seventy nations, of which you are the best and the dearest to Allah.'

To be the best and the dearest to Allah ﷻ does not happen by simply claiming it. We have to be worthy of it by following the guidance of our leader, *Rasul Allah* ﷺ. We can measure how worthy we are by asking ourselves, when we see things going on around us, are we enjoining good or discouraging evil? This concept is not easy for everyone to put into practise on a communal basis, but at the very least, everybody can work on himself or herself and maybe guide those closest to us.

To be the best *ummah* and the best nation is based on two conditions; the concept of enjoining good and secondly, forbidding evil.

May Allah ﷻ teach us what is beneficial for us and may Allah ﷻ help us to practise what we learn.

Points to reflect on:

- Holding onto Allah's ﷻ rope requires staying connected to the Qur'an: how are we doing with this and how can we improve?
- To be the 'best of nations' means enjoining good and forbidding evil. What are the opportunities in my daily life to do this; personally, in my family, in my local community and then beyond?
- Staying united in the *ummah* starts with ourselves in our local communities. We can look at how welcoming our *masajids* are, for example, to different sections of society; the elderly, new Muslims, the disabled, single mothers and so on.
- To be worthy of being dearest to Allah ﷻ includes following the guidance of *Rasul Allah* ﷺ. We need to check on our practise of the Sunnah and strive to learn and practise more of it.

وَٱلْمُؤْمِنُونَ وَٱلْمُؤْمِنَٰتُ بَعْضُهُمْ أَوْلِيَآءُ بَعْضٍ ۚ يَأْمُرُونَ بِٱلْمَعْرُوفِ وَيَنْهَوْنَ عَنِ
ٱلْمُنكَرِ وَيُقِيمُونَ ٱلصَّلَوٰةَ وَيُؤْتُونَ ٱلزَّكَوٰةَ وَيُطِيعُونَ ٱللَّهَ وَرَسُولَهُۥٓ ۚ أُو۟لَٰٓئِكَ
سَيَرْحَمُهُمُ ٱللَّهُ ۗ إِنَّ ٱللَّهَ عَزِيزٌ حَكِيمٌ ۝

The believers, both men and women, support each other; they order what is right and forbid what is wrong; they keep up the prayer and pay the prescribed alms; they obey God and His Messenger. God will give His mercy to such people: God is Almighty and Wise.

(*Tawbah* 9: 71)

Chapter 13

WHICH WOMEN ARE NAMED IN THE QUR'AN?

In the journey of discovering what the Qur'an says on life's important subjects, we come to the question of women. Does the Qur'an mention women? Many women are mentioned in the Qur'an by name or by reference. For example, the wife of *Sayyidina Ibrahim – Haajar* and the wife of Al-Aziz in Chapter Yusuf. We have *Hawwa*, although her name is not mentioned specifically in the Qur'an. We also have the mother of *Sayyidina* Musa and the daughters of *Sayyidina* Shu'ayb found in these prophets' narratives.

In this chapter we will discover what Allah revealed about them in the Qur'an.

Mothers in the Qur'an

The first category is mothers in the Qur'an. A well-known example is the mother of *Sayyida* Maryam who begged Allah to give her a righteous child.

إِذْ قَالَتِ امْرَأَتُ عِمْرَانَ رَبِّ إِنِّي نَذَرْتُ لَكَ مَا فِي بَطْنِي مُحَرَّرًا فَتَقَبَّلْ
مِنِّي ۖ إِنَّكَ أَنتَ السَّمِيعُ الْعَلِيمُ

The wife of Imran said, "My Lord, I have dedicated what is in my womb, to You, so accept it from me; You are the Hearer and Knower of all."

(*al-'Imrān* 3:35)

Her story continues:

فَلَمَّا وَضَعَتْهَا قَالَتْ رَبِّ إِنِّي وَضَعْتُهَا أُنثَىٰ

And when she delivered her, she said, "My Lord, I have delivered a female,"

(*al-'Imrān* 3:36)

When she said that the girl is not like the boy or the woman is not like the man, it meant in the context of this *ayah*, that they are not the same in terms of their service in the temple. In those times, only the male child was handed to the temple to dedicate his life. However, the mother of Maryam wanted a baby who would serve Allah. In response Allah tells us:

فَتَقَبَّلَهَا رَبُّهَا بِقَبُولٍ حَسَنٍ

Her Lord accepted her with a gracious reception.

(*al-'Imrān* 3:37)

When *Sayyida* Maryam ﷺ was dedicated to the temple to worship, *Sayyidina* Zakaria ﷺ took care of her. كُلَّمَا دَخَلَ عَلَيْهَا زَكَرِيَّا ٱلْمِحْرَابَ Every time he entered her *mihrab* – prayer niche, وَجَدَ عِندَهَا رِزْقًا He found she had sustenance. قَالَ يَـٰمَرْيَمُ أَنَّىٰ لَكِ هَـٰذَا He asked, Maryam ﷺ, where did this come from? قَالَتْ هُوَ مِنْ عِندِ ٱللَّهِ She replied, it's from Allah ﷻ إِنَّ ٱللَّهَ يَرْزُقُ مَن يَشَآءُ بِغَيْرِ حِسَابٍ. Allah ﷻ gives sustenance to whom He wills without accounting for it. The answer to Maryam's mother's *du'a* resulted in her becoming the most honoured mother in history – the mother of *Isa* ﷺ.

What is the message here for us and all women? Make *du'a* to Allah ﷻ even before one gets married, for a righteous child, as one should continue to do when married and pregnant. Allah ﷻ shows us how the *du'a* for a righteous child, resulted in the life of *Sayyida* Maryam ﷺ. We are reminded that Allah ﷻ listens, He hears, and He gives the way that pleases people, but most importantly He gives in a way that He knows is best for us.

The second mothers' example in the Qur'an is the mother who put her trust in Allah ﷻ completely: the mother of *Sayyidina* Musa ﷺ. In *Surah al Qasas* – The Stories, Allah ﷻ tells us:

وَأَوْحَيْنَآ إِلَىٰٓ أُمِّ مُوسَىٰٓ أَنْ أَرْضِعِيهِ ۖ فَإِذَا خِفْتِ عَلَيْهِ فَأَلْقِيهِ فِى ٱلْيَمِّ وَلَا تَخَافِى وَلَا تَحْزَنِىٓ ۖ إِنَّا رَآدُّوهُ إِلَيْكِ وَجَاعِلُوهُ مِنَ ٱلْمُرْسَلِينَ

And We inspired the mother of Moses: "Nurse him; but when you fear for him, put him into the river, and do not fear, nor be sad. We will return him to you, and will make him one of the messengers."

(*al-Qaṣaṣ* 28:7-8)

When we think about her situation, we question how many mothers could do this? How many can take their newborn baby and put him in a basket in the river? Musa's ﷺ mother not only believed in Allah ﷻ, but she had certainty that Allah ﷻ would bring her baby back to her. The story continues to show us how amazingly Allah ﷻ plans things for each one of us. A maid from the enemy – *Fir'aun's* household, who was killing baby boys out of fear of them taking his throne, picked up baby Musa ﷺ and took him back to the wife of *Fir'aun*. Aasiya ﷺ, the noble wife of this tyrant said:

"Here is a delight of the eye to me and to you. Do not kill him. Maybe he will prove useful for us, or we may adopt him as a son." They were unaware of the end of it all.

(al-Qasas 28:9)

At the same time, we are told about the condition of the mother of Musa ﷺ and how her heart became empty and she was distressed, and she would have told people 'the boy in the house of *Fir'aun* is mine.' The story continues in the Qur'an, where we learn:

وَأَصْبَحَ فُؤَادُ أُمِّ مُوسَىٰ فَـٰرِغًا إِن كَادَتْ لَتُبْدِىْ بِهِ لَوْ لَآ أَنْ رَّبَطْنَا عَلَىٰ قَلْبِهَا لِتَكُوْنَ مِنَ الْمُؤْمِنِيْنَ.

On the other hand, the heart of Moses' mother was sorely distressed. Had We not strengthened her heart that she might have full faith (in Our promise), she would have disclosed the secret.

(*al-Qasas* 28:10)

Allah ﷻ gave her the strength which is one of the things we learn from this event. Whenever we feel weak, we should turn to Him and put our trust in Allah ﷻ. He will keep us strong. Allah ﷻ planned a way to bring Musa's ﷺ mother relief as the following verses narrate:

وَقَالَتْ لِأُخْتِهِۦ قُصِّيهِ فَبَصُرَتْ بِهِۦ عَن جُنُبٍ وَهُمْ لَا يَشْعُرُونَ ۝ وَحَرَّمْنَا عَلَيْهِ ٱلْمَرَاضِعَ مِن قَبْلُ فَقَالَتْ هَلْ أَدُلُّكُمْ عَلَىٰٓ أَهْلِ بَيْتٍ يَكْفُلُونَهُۥ لَكُمْ وَهُمْ لَهُۥ نَـٰصِحُونَ ۝ فَرَدَدْنَـٰهُ إِلَىٰٓ أُمِّهِۦ كَىْ تَقَرَّ عَيْنُهَا وَلَا تَحْزَنَ وَلِتَعْلَمَ أَنَّ وَعْدَ ٱللَّهِ حَقٌّ وَلَـٰكِنَّ أَكْثَرَهُمْ لَا يَعْلَمُونَ ۝

She told the sister of Moses: "Follow him." So she kept watch over him unperceived (by the enemies). And We had already forbidden the breasts of the nurses for the child. (So seeing the girl) said: "Shall I direct you to the people of a household that will rear him with utter sincerity?"

Thus did We restore Moses to his mother that her eyes might be comforted and she might not grieve, and realise that the promise of Allah was true. But most people are unaware of this.

(*al-Qasas* 28:11-13)

We are told here to have faith in the plan of Allah ﷻ, as Allah ﷻ plans in ways that are different to what we expect. In this case Allah ﷻ decreed that Musa عليه السلام would refuse every breastfeeding woman who came to nurse him until his own mother was brought back to feed him. In this way, his mother's grief and sadness was replaced with happiness and comfort, realising that 'the promise of Allah ﷻ is true.' The message to all women is to have faith in Allah ﷻ, rely on Him and know that whatever Allah ﷻ plans has good in it for us.

Wives in the Qur'an

Allah ﷻ gives examples of specific wives in the Qur'an. In the following *ayah* two wives are given as an example of those whom Allah ﷻ did not praise, for the reasons found here:

ضَرَبَ اللَّهُ مَثَلًا لِّلَّذِينَ كَفَرُوا امْرَأَتَ نُوحٍ وَامْرَأَتَ لُوطٍ ۖ كَانَتَا تَحْتَ عَبْدَيْنِ مِنْ عِبَادِنَا صَالِحَيْنِ فَخَانَتَاهُمَا فَلَمْ يُغْنِيَا عَنْهُمَا مِنَ اللَّهِ شَيْئًا وَقِيلَ ادْخُلَا النَّارَ مَعَ الدَّاخِلِينَ ﴿١٠﴾

Allah illustrates an example for those who disbelieve: the wife of Noah and the wife of Lot. They were wedded to two of Our righteous servants, but they betrayed them. They availed them nothing against Allah, and it was said, "Enter the Fire with those who are entering."

(*al-Taḥrīm* 66:10)

The wife of Noah and the wife of Lut are examples of those who betrayed their righteous husbands. How did they betray them? *Sayyidina* Noah's عليه السلام wife, her name was Wahila, used to say to his people that her husband had lost his mind. The wife of *Sayyidina* Lut عليه السلام, used to tell people there were men in her house, when the angels or when men visited them. With the *fitna* of the society she was in, this was a betrayal of her guests. The lesson here, is that regardless of one's family, it's one's own work and deeds that will decide the fate of a person. In the case of these two women, their destination was *Jahannam* – Hell Fire, in spite of them coming from the most righteous homes, because they disobeyed Allah ﷻ and did things they shouldn't have done.

Aasiya, the wife of Pharoah

In the next verse from *Surah al-Tahrim* we are given a contrasting example. It continues:

وَضَرَبَ اللَّهُ مَثَلًا لِلَّذِينَ آمَنُوا امْرَأَتَ فِرْعَوْنَ إِذْ قَالَتْ رَبِّ ابْنِ لِي عِنْدَكَ بَيْتًا
فِي الْجَنَّةِ وَنَجِّنِي مِنْ فِرْعَوْنَ وَعَمَلِهِ وَنَجِّنِي مِنَ الْقَوْمِ الظَّالِمِينَ

Allah illustrates an example for those who believe: the wife of Pharaoh, when she said, "My Lord! Build for me a house in Paradise near You, and rescue me from Pharaoh and his works, and rescue me from the wrongdoing people."

(*al-Taḥrīm* 66:10-11)

The wife of Pharaoh, Aasiya living with *Fir'aun*, prayed to Allah ﷻ for a house near to Him in *Jannah*. It is said that *Fir'aun* was so upset with her when she believed in Allah ﷻ that he laid her down in the sun and used to torture her. When he left her, Allah ﷻ sent a cloud to shade her and angels came to see her and that's when she made the *du'a* and died. It is narrated that she was very happy and smiling at this time because she would be elevated to be with Allah ﷻ.

This is a lesson for the wives who are living in difficult marriages and who are struggling, to obey Allah ﷻ and stay connected with Him. Aasiya was living with Allah's ﷻ enemy but kept her faith. In this chapter the examples of some mothers and wives mentioned in the Qur'an were covered, amongst the many women whose narratives appear in various *surahs* in the next chapter we will discover more details about women who had power and what the Qur'an says about them.

Point to reflect on:

- The Qur'an honours women, with the fourth chapter called *al-Nisa* – The Women. Many women are mentioned in the Qur'an, including mothers, wives, and others whose stories teach us valuable lessons.

- Making *du'a* for righteous children is encouraged. The mother of Maryam made *du'a* before she gave birth, showing us how powerful and important it is to ask Allah ﷻ for righteous children early on

- Mothers with strong faith such as the mother of Musa ﷺ trusted Allah ﷻ completely, and was given strength and relief from Him during her most testing time.

- Each person is responsible for their actions. The wives of the two prophets, Nūḥ and Lūṭ ﷺ, are examples of being close to a righteous person will not help us if we don't obey Allah ﷻ ourselves.

- Allah ﷻ rewards patience and belief: Aasiya ﷺ, the wife of Pharaoh, shows us how a woman can stay strong in her faith. Her connection with Allah ﷻ brought her the ultimate reward of *Jannah*.

إِنَّ ٱلْمُسْلِمِينَ وَٱلْمُسْلِمَٰتِ وَٱلْمُؤْمِنِينَ وَٱلْمُؤْمِنَٰتِ وَٱلْقَٰنِتِينَ وَٱلْقَٰنِتَٰتِ
وَٱلصَّٰدِقِينَ وَٱلصَّٰدِقَٰتِ وَٱلصَّٰبِرِينَ وَٱلصَّٰبِرَٰتِ وَٱلْخَٰشِعِينَ وَٱلْخَٰشِعَٰتِ
وَٱلْمُتَصَدِّقِينَ وَٱلْمُتَصَدِّقَٰتِ وَٱلصَّٰٓئِمِينَ وَٱلصَّٰٓئِمَٰتِ وَٱلْحَٰفِظِينَ فُرُوجَهُمْ
وَٱلْحَٰفِظَٰتِ وَٱلذَّٰكِرِينَ ٱللَّهَ كَثِيرًا وَٱلذَّٰكِرَٰتِ أَعَدَّ ٱللَّهُ لَهُم مَّغْفِرَةً وَأَجْرًا عَظِيمًا ۝

For men and women who are devoted to God- believing men and women, obedient men and women, truthful men and women, steadfast men and women, humble men and women, charitable men and women, fasting men and women, chaste men and women, men and women who remember God often- God has prepared forgiveness and a rich reward.

(*al-Ahzab* 33:35)

Chapter 14

ARE THERE ANY POWERFUL WOMEN IN THE QUR'AN?

In the previous chapter, we discovered what the Qur'an says about the wives and mothers of certain Prophets. Are these the only women mentioned, or are there anymore? There are other significant women Allah ﷻ draws our attention to and in this chapter we will discover a powerful woman who became a believer. Who was she, and what was her story?

The Qur'an gives us a thorough account of the Queen of Sheba, Bilqees. Allah ﷻ covers her story in *Surah an-Naml*, in relation to *Sayyidina* Sulaiman ﵇ and his kingdom. We start at the scene where *Sayyidina* Sulaiman ﵇ notices one of his birds is absent:

وَتَفَقَّدَ ٱلطَّيْرَ فَقَالَ مَا لِيَ لَآ أَرَى ٱلْهُدْهُدَ أَمْ كَانَ مِنَ ٱلْغَآئِبِينَ ۝ لَأُعَذِّبَنَّهُۥ عَذَابًا
شَدِيدًا أَوْ لَأَا۟ذْبَحَنَّهُۥٓ أَوْ لَيَأْتِيَنِّى بِسُلْطَـٰنٍ مُّبِينٍ ۝ فَمَكَثَ غَيْرَ بَعِيدٍ فَقَالَ
أَحَطتُ بِمَا لَمْ تُحِطْ بِهِۦ وَجِئْتُكَ مِن سَبَإٍۭ بِنَبَإٍ يَقِينٍ ۝
إِنِّى وَجَدتُّ ٱمْرَأَةً تَمْلِكُهُمْ وَأُوتِيَتْ مِن كُلِّ شَىْءٍ وَلَهَا عَرْشٌ عَظِيمٌ ۝
وَجَدتُّهَا وَقَوْمَهَا يَسْجُدُونَ لِلشَّمْسِ مِن دُونِ ٱللَّهِ وَزَيَّنَ لَهُمُ ٱلشَّيْطَـٰنُ أَعْمَـٰلَهُمْ
فَصَدَّهُمْ عَنِ ٱلسَّبِيلِ فَهُمْ لَا يَهْتَدُونَ ۝

Solomon inspected the birds and said, 'Why do I not see the hoopoe? Is he absent? I will punish him severely, or kill him, unless he brings me a convincing excuse for his absence.' But the hoopoe did not stay away long: he came and said, 'I have learned something you did not know: I come to you from Sheba with clear news. I found a woman ruling over the people, who has been given a share of everything (power)- she has a magnificent throne, [but] I found that she and her people prostrating to the sun instead of God. Satan has made their deeds seem alluring to them, and diverted them from the right path: they cannot find the right path. Shouldn't they prostrate only to Allah, Who discloses whatever is hidden in the Heavens and the Earth, and Who knows whatever you choose either to conceal or reveal? There is no go but Allah, the Lord of the mighty Throne.'

(*al-Naml* 27:20-26)

Sayyidina Sulaiman ﵇ questioned the Hoopoe to make sure he was telling the truth, then he instructed this bird to take a letter to the Queen and wait to see what the reply will be:

قَالَ سَنَنظُرُ أَصَدَقْتَ أَمْ كُنتَ مِنَ ٱلْكَـٰذِبِينَ ۝
ٱذْهَب بِّكِتَـٰبِى هَـٰذَا فَأَلْقِهْ إِلَيْهِمْ ثُمَّ تَوَلَّ عَنْهُمْ فَٱنظُرْ مَاذَا يَرْجِعُونَ ۝

"We shall see if you are telling the truth or lying.
Then go with this letter of mine and make sure they receive it, then move a little way from them and see what response they come back with."

(*al-Naml* 27:27-28)

At this point in the Qur'an's narrative, Allah ﷻ starts telling us who Bilqees, the Queen of Sheba, is and her personality unfolds through the way she communicates with her emissaries. We are shown the Queen of Sheba is a woman of strength and wisdom. The letter from Prophet Sulaiman ﷺ is delivered to Bilqees:

انَّهُۥ مِن سُلَيۡمَـٰنَ،
. وَإِنَّهُۥ بِسۡمِ ٱللَّهِ ٱلرَّحۡمَـٰنِ ٱلرَّحِيمِ.
أَلَّا تَعۡلُواْ عَلَىَّ وَأۡتُونِى مُسۡلِمِينَ.

The Queen said: "My lords, I have received a gracious letter.
It is from Sulaiman and reads: 'In the name of Allah, the Kind, the Caring.
Do not think yourselves above me, but come to me in submission.' "

(*al-Naml* 27:29-31)

This is the only chapter in the Qur'an that has two بِسۡمِ ٱللَّهِ ٱلرَّحۡمَـٰنِ ٱلرَّحِيمِ. – *Bismillah al Rahman al Rahim* in it. The letter from *Sayyidina* Sulaiman ﷺ states his recommendations: don't act with arrogance and submit to what I am telling you, come to faith as a Muslim. As a queen with power, what would one expect her reaction to be? She proceeded with wisdom:

قَالَتۡ يَـٰٓأَيُّهَا ٱلۡمَلَؤُاْ أَفۡتُونِى فِىٓ أَمۡرِى مَا كُنتُ قَاطِعَةً أَمۡرًا حَتَّىٰ تَشۡهَدُونِ۝

So she asked, "My lords, advise me in this matter. I don't make any decisions without your presence and advice.".

In response, they said:

قَالُواْ نَحۡنُ أُوْلُواْ قُوَّةٍ وَأُوْلُواْ بَأۡسٍ شَدِيدٍ وَٱلۡأَمۡرُ إِلَيۡكِ فَٱنظُرِى مَاذَا تَأۡمُرِينَ۝

"We possess power and military might but the final decision rests with you; tell us what to do."

(*al-Naml* 27: 32-33)

The Queen of Sheba was a woman of wisdom who consulted those around her, and was willing to listen to the advice. Although she was a queen, she wasn't the type of person who insisted on making all the decisions by herself. Instead, she shared her concern and worry:

قَالَتْ إِنَّ ٱلْمُلُوكَ إِذَا دَخَلُوا۟ قَرْيَةً أَفْسَدُوهَا وَجَعَلُوٓا۟ أَعِزَّةَ أَهْلِهَآ أَذِلَّةً ۖ وَكَذَٰلِكَ يَفْعَلُونَ .

She said "When Kings enter a city, they lay waste to it and humiliate its nobility; that is their way."
(*al-Naml* 27: 34)

The letter did not make her worried, it was the thought and experience of what powerful rulers do when they overtake a city. What do they do? They spread mischief and humiliate those in power. So Bilqees thought about trying something new. She said,

وَإِنِّى مُرْسِلَةٌ إِلَيْهِم بِهَدِيَّةٍ فَنَاظِرَةٌۢ بِمَ يَرْجِعُ ٱلْمُرْسَلُونَ ۝

"I'm going to send them a gift, and I'm going to wait and see what the envoys come back with."
(*al-Naml* 27: 35)

Why did she do this? Her reason was to distinguish if Sulaiman ﷺ was a king or a Prophet as she didn't know. If he was a King, he would take the gift, and if he was a Prophet, he would refuse gifts. So the Queen used her wisdom and intelligence to learn who Sulaiman ﷺ really was. When her emissaries reached *Sayyidina* Sulaiman ﷺ, he responded directly:

فَلَمَّا جَآءَ سُلَيْمَٰنَ قَالَ أَتُمِدُّونَنِ بِمَالٍ فَمَآ ءَاتَىٰنِۦَ ٱللَّهُ خَيْرٌ مِّمَّآ ءَاتَىٰكُم بَلْ أَنتُم بِهَدِيَّتِكُمْ تَفْرَحُونَ ۝

"Are you offering me wealth? What Allah has given me is far better than what He has given you. Only the likes of you rejoice in such gifts."
(*al-Naml* 27:36)

His answer conveyed his thoughts: I am not going to be lured by money to change what I am supposed to do, hence I don't need these gifts. *Sayyidina* Sulaiman ﷺ had a huge kingdom and wealth of his own. Instead, he sent Queen Bilqees's envoy with the following message:

ٱرْجِعْ إِلَيْهِمْ فَلَنَأْتِيَنَّهُم بِجُنُودٍ لَّا قِبَلَ لَهُم بِهَا وَلَنُخْرِجَنَّهُم
مِّنْهَآ أَذِلَّةً وَهُمْ صَٰغِرُونَ ۝

"Go back to your people and tell them We shall come with armies that they can't face, and we shall expel them from their city, humiliated and disgraced.'

(*al-Naml* 27:37)

Then addressing his own courtiers, he asks:

قَالَ يَٰٓأَيُّهَا ٱلْمَلَؤُا۟ أَيُّكُمْ يَأْتِينِى بِعَرْشِهَا قَبْلَ أَن يَأْتُونِى مُسْلِمِينَ ۝

"Who can bring me her throne before they come to me in submission?"

(*al-Naml* 27:38)

The Queen possessed a great throne: 120 feet long (36.5 m), 60 feet wide (13.29 m) and 45 feet high (13.72 m). It was very heavy and was made of gold and silver, encrusted with pearls and a lot of gems. Bilqees was a woman in possession of great wealth.

قَالَ عِفْرِيتٌ مِّنَ ٱلْجِنِّ أَنَا۠ ءَاتِيكَ بِهِۦ قَبْلَ أَن تَقُومَ مِن
مَّقَامِكَ ۖ وَإِنِّى عَلَيْهِ لَقَوِىٌّ أَمِينٌ ۝
قَالَ ٱلَّذِى عِندَهُۥ عِلْمٌ مِّنَ ٱلْكِتَٰبِ أَنَا۠ ءَاتِيكَ بِهِۦ قَبْلَ أَن يَرْتَدَّ إِلَيْكَ طَرْفُكَ ۚ فَلَمَّا
رَءَاهُ مُسْتَقِرًّا عِندَهُۥ قَالَ هَٰذَا مِن فَضْلِ رَبِّى لِيَبْلُوَنِىٓ ءَأَشْكُرُ أَمْ أَكْفُرُ ۖ وَمَن
شَكَرَ فَإِنَّمَا يَشْكُرُ لِنَفْسِهِۦ ۖ وَمَن كَفَرَ فَإِنَّ رَبِّى غَنِىٌّ كَرِيمٌ ۝

A powerful and crafty jinn replied, 'I will bring it to you before you can even rise from your place. I am strong and trustworthy enough,' but one of them who had some knowledge of the Scripture said, 'I will bring it to you in the twinkling of an eye.' When Sulaiman saw it set before him, he said, 'This is a favour from my Lord, to test whether I am grateful or not: if anyone is grateful, it is for his own good, if anyone is ungrateful, then my Lord is Self-sufficient and Most generous.'

(*al-Naml* 27:39-40)

What happened next was that Allah ﷻ made the throne come through the Earth quickly and in front of *Sayyidina* Sulaiman ﷺ. When he opened his eyes and saw it in front of him, he responded in a Prophetic manner:

قَالَ نَكِّرُواْ لَهَا عَرْشَهَا نَنظُرْ أَتَهْتَدِىٓ أَمْ تَكُونُ مِنَ ٱلَّذِينَ لَا يَهْتَدُونَ

He said "Disguise her throne so that we can see if she is guided or not."

(*al-Naml* 27:41)

We can compare *Sayyidina* Sulaiman's ﷺ response with that of Qarun who had extensive wealth, but was ungrateful to Allah ﷻ, and proclaimed his wealth was because of his own knowledge (*al-Qasas* 28:78). What the Qur'an is teaching us is that being grateful benefits ourselves, as Allah ﷻ is not in need of anything from us.

The story continues when Bilquees sees the throne.

فَلَمَّا جَآءَتْ قِيلَ أَهَٰكَذَا عَرْشُكِ ۖ قَالَتْ كَأَنَّهُۥ هُوَ ۚ وَأُوتِينَا
ٱلْعِلْمَ مِن قَبْلِهَا وَكُنَّا مُسْلِمِينَ ۝

After arriving, the Queen was asked "Is your throne like this?" She said, "It looks just like it." And Sulaiman said "We were given prior knowledge and we submitted to Allah. What had previously stopped her was what she used to worship beside Allah, as she came from a disbelieving community."

(*al-Naml* 27:41-43)

Bilquees was astute and said this could resemble her throne. Yet in spite of her wisdom, she was a disbeliever because of the people surrounding her. This reminds us of the power and influence of one's company. *Sayyidina* Sulaiman ﷺ invited Bilquees into his palace. This palace was huge with floors made of clear crystal which resembled water.

قِيلَ لَهَا ٱدْخُلِى ٱلصَّرْحَ ۖ فَلَمَّا رَأَتْهُ حَسِبَتْهُ لُجَّةً وَكَشَفَتْ عَن سَاقَيْهَا ۚ قَالَ إِنَّهُۥ
صَرْحٌ مُّمَرَّدٌ مِّن قَوَارِيرَ ۗ قَالَتْ رَبِّ إِنِّى ظَلَمْتُ نَفْسِى وَأَسْلَمْتُ مَعَ سُلَيْمَٰنَ لِلَّهِ
رَبِّ ٱلْعَٰلَمِينَ ۝

Then it was said to her, 'Enter the hall,' but when she saw it, she thought it was a deep pool of water, and bared her legs. Sulaiman explained, 'It is just a hall paved with glass,'. When she saw that, and saw her throne she said, 'My Lord, I have wronged myself: I devote myself, with Sulaiman, to Allah, the Lord of the Worlds.

(*al-Naml* 27:44)

This narration covered at length in this *surah* teaches us many lessons. Firstly, whether it's a man or a woman, Allah ﷻ bestows power and one who it is given to should not become arrogant. Secondly, if consulting others and listening to their opinion is a wise strategy. Thirdly, if we find out we are wrong, we should admit our mistake, submit and ask Allah ﷻ for forgiveness, exactly as Bilquees did. Although she was a woman with authority, she was misguided by her people to prostrate to the sun. However, when she saw the miracle of how her throne moved across the world, she didn't deny the truth. On the contrary she said, '*Ya Allah, I wronged myself and I submit to Sulaiman*'.

May Allah ﷻ make us follow the example of Bilquees. May Allah ﷻ make us of those who, when they read the Qur'an, not only learn but practise it and come closer to Allah ﷻ. Amīn.

Points to reflect on:

- Bilqees consulted her advisors and was open to their views. Taking advice from trustworthy people in our daily lives prevents arrogance and encourages humility.
- Reflect with wisdom. When Bilqees wanted to understand whether *Sayyidina* Sulaiman ﷺ was a prophet or king, she responded with giving a gift in order to learn the truth about him. This took reflection and intelligence to respond appropriately and teaches us to consider new situations.
- How do we view wealth and power? Prophet Sulaiman ﷺ had a great kingdom and power of all types of creatures, yet he remained focused on worshipping Allah ﷻ.
- All wealth and status is from Allah ﷻ and is only useful if we can use it to please Him and remain grateful and steadfast.
- This story reminds us that our company impacts our beliefs. If we choose believers as friends and companions, this will help our journey towards Allah ﷻ as they are on the same path.
- How do we deal with mistakes? Everyone will make mistakes in life. Having the humility to admit our mistakes and turn to Allah ﷻ sincerely is the key, as He is *Al Ghafir – Al Ghafur.*

وَٱصْبِرْ نَفْسَكَ مَعَ ٱلَّذِينَ يَدْعُونَ رَبَّهُم بِٱلْغَدَوٰةِ وَٱلْعَشِىِّ يُرِيدُونَ وَجْهَهُۥ ۖ وَلَا تَعْدُ
عَيْنَاكَ عَنْهُمْ تُرِيدُ زِينَةَ ٱلْحَيَوٰةِ ٱلدُّنْيَا ۖ وَلَا تُطِعْ مَنْ أَغْفَلْنَا قَلْبَهُۥ عَن ذِكْرِنَا وَٱتَّبَعَ
هَوَىٰهُ وَكَانَ أَمْرُهُۥ فُرُطًا ۝

Content yourself with those who pray to their Sustainer morning and evening, seeking His approval, and do not let your eyes turn away from them out of desire for the attractions of this worldly life: do not yield to those whose hearts We have made heedless of Our Quran, those who follow their own low desires, those whose ways are beyond all bounds.

(*al-Kahf* 18:28)

Chapter 15

DOES THE QUR'AN TALK ABOUT OUR DRESS CODE?

As a community of women and men living together on this Earth, there are many questions about what makes us unique. One of our differences to the rest of Allah's ﷻ creation is the need for clothing. Does Allah ﷻ address how we should dress in the Qur'an? He does clearly give us guidelines on how men and women should dress.

In *Surah al-A'raf*, the Heights, Allah ﷻ addresses us all 'Ya, Bani Adam'; a call to all the children of Adam, Muslims, non-Muslims, everyone living before us and coming after us:

يَا بَنِي آدَمَ قَدْ أَنْزَلْنَا عَلَيْكُمْ لِبَاسًا يُوَارِي سَوْآتِكُمْ وَرِيشًا

O children of Adam, We have provided you clothing to cover your nakedness and as an adornment.

(*al-Aʿrāf* 7:26)

Here, Allah ﷻ tells us clothing is to cover our private parts, and, as the word وَرِيشًا *'r'isha'* shows, clothing is given to beautify us which comes under the things that are permitted for us.

Garment of *Taqwa*

This *ayah* continues and after Allah ﷻ sets out the main purpose of our dress, He then places a spiritual alternative beside the practical reasons for clothing. He says:

وَلِبَاسُ التَّقْوَىٰ ذَٰلِكَ خَيْرٌ

ذَٰلِكَ خَيْرٌ ذَٰلِكَ مِنْ ءَايَـٰتِ ٱللَّهِ لَعَلَّهُمْ يَذَّكَّرُونَ ۝

But the clothing of righteousness—that is best,
This is one of God's signs so people will take heed.

(*al-Aʿrāf* 7:26)

The garment of *taqwa* here is described as a sign of Allah ﷻ and the best of clothing. This gives us something to reflect on and draw lessons from. This وَلِبَاسُ التَّقْوَىٰ garment of *taqwa* is encouraging consciousness of Allah ﷻ in order to guide us in all our choices. It is something that should be very close to us, just like our clothing and should affect us positively, making us constantly aware of Allah ﷻ, remembering and obeying Him.

Allah ﷻ is then explicit in what He wants us to learn in the next verse:

يَا بَنِي آدَمَ لَا يَفْتِنَنَّكُمُ الشَّيْطَانُ كَمَا أَخْرَجَ أَبَوَيْكُم مِّنَ الْجَنَّةِ
يَنزِعُ عَنْهُمَا لِبَاسَهُمَا لِيُرِيَهُمَا سَوْآتِهِمَا

O Children of Adam! Let not Satan seduce you, as he drove your parents out of the Garden, stripping them of their garments to show them their nakedness.

(*al-Aʿrāf* 7:27)

Once again, يَـٰبَنِىٓ ءَادَمَ. all of us, the children of Adam are being addressed and are being reminded, do not let *Shaytan* lure you. In chapter four we covered why we didn't stay in *Jannah*, and part of the discussion there was about *Shaytan's* tricks and deceptive ways. In *Jannah*, *Shaytan* made them disobey Allah ﷻ, and as a result of the disobedience to Allah ﷻ, they became aware of being unclothed and a feeling of immodesty came over them. Human nature dislikes immodesty and human beings have the instinct of wanting to be clothed.

The concept of *Hayah*

Allah's ﷻ focus is always on something called *hayah*, which means inner and outer modesty and is usually related to modesty in clothing. Allah ﷻ is telling us, not to be deceived by *Shaytan* who lured our parents towards immortality by eating from the forbidden tree. *Iblis* knew if they disobeyed, their nakedness would be exposed. So linking the story of Adam & Hawwa in *Jannah*, with clothing and modesty is a reminder to us all to be careful to maintain our modesty.

Prophet Muhammad ﷺ said 'Every religion has a defining characteristic. And the single defining characteristic of our religion is modesty – *hayah*.'

Men and women's dress code:

We find further details in *Surah al-Nur*, the chapter called Light, where Allah ﷻ specifies about the dress code. For the man, he said two things:

قُل لِّلْمُؤْمِنِينَ يَغُضُّوا۟ مِنْ أَبْصَـٰرِهِمْ وَيَحْفَظُوا۟ فُرُوجَهُمْ ۚ ذَٰلِكَ أَزْكَىٰ لَهُمْ ۗ إِنَّ ٱللَّهَ
خَبِيرٌۢ بِمَا يَصْنَعُونَ ۝

Say to the believing man, lower your gaze because that will help in the conduct between the two genders. Guard their private parts including in the dress code. Allah is all aware of what they are doing.

(*al-Nur* 24:30)

When it comes to the woman, Allah ﷻ goes into more details. Why is this? It's because for women, taking care of their appearance is a normal part of their nature. Allah ﷻ beautified them and He addresses them in the same way, starting with:

وَقُل لِّلْمُؤْمِنَٰتِ يَغْضُضْنَ مِنْ أَبْصَٰرِهِنَّ وَيَحْفَظْنَ فُرُوجَهُنَّ وَلَا يُبْدِينَ زِينَتَهُنَّ إِلَّا مَا ظَهَرَ مِنْهَا ۖ وَلْيَضْرِبْنَ بِخُمُرِهِنَّ عَلَىٰ جُيُوبِهِنَّ ۖ

And tell the believing women to restrain their looks, and to guard their privates, and not display their beauty except what is apparent thereof, and to draw their coverings over their breasts.

(*al-Nūr* 24:31)

The majority of scholars say it is alright for the face and hands not to be covered. There are other scholars who interpret that the face needs to be covered too. Allah ﷻ continues after this to give more details about the head covering:

وَلْيَضْرِبْنَ بِخُمُرِهِنَّ عَلَىٰ جُيُوبِهِنَّ ۖ

and to draw their coverings over their breasts.

What is *al-khimar*? *Khimar* is from the word *khamr*, which means 'something that covers'. And in that time, *khimar* was classed as the head cover, which they didn't call *hijab*, as we do now. But at that time when the Qur'an was being revealed, they used to wear it very loosely on the head in a way that didn't cover their chest or neck. Allah ﷻ says in this verse to draw the head cover and cover the whole part from the neck down to the cleavage of the breast: وَلْيَضْرِبْنَ بِخُمُرِهِنَّ. This is what the hijab is; covering the hair and chest. What a woman does to look beautiful is not *haram*, but there are limitations on who can see her hair and beautified state.

Allah ﷻ continues with details and gives counsel not to show one's beauty except to the following people who are all *mahrams* – meaning men that a woman cannot marry.

وَلَا يُبْدِينَ زِينَتَهُنَّ إِلَّا لِبُعُولَتِهِنَّ أَوْ ءَابَآئِهِنَّ أَوْ ءَابَآءِ بُعُولَتِهِنَّ أَوْ أَبْنَآئِهِنَّ أَوْ أَبْنَآءِ
بُعُولَتِهِنَّ أَوْ إِخْوَٰنِهِنَّ أَوْ بَنِىٓ إِخْوَٰنِهِنَّ أَوْ بَنِىٓ أَخَوَٰتِهِنَّ أَوْ نِسَآئِهِنَّ أَوْ مَا مَلَكَتْ
أَيْمَٰنُهُنَّ أَوِ ٱلتَّٰبِعِينَ غَيْرِ أُو۟لِى ٱلْإِرْبَةِ مِنَ ٱلرِّجَالِ أَوِ ٱلطِّفْلِ ٱلَّذِينَ لَمْ يَظْهَرُوا۟
عَلَىٰ عَوْرَٰتِ ٱلنِّسَآءِ ۖ وَلَا يَضْرِبْنَ بِأَرْجُلِهِنَّ لِيُعْلَمَ مَا يُخْفِينَ مِن زِينَتِهِنَّ ۚ وَتُوبُوٓا۟
إِلَى ٱللَّهِ جَمِيعًا أَيُّهَ ٱلْمُؤْمِنُونَ لَعَلَّكُمْ تُفْلِحُونَ ۝

...they should let their headscarves fall to cover their necklines and not reveal their charms except to their husbands, their fathers, their husbands' fathers, their sons, their husbands' sons, their brothers, their brothers' sons, their sisters' sons, their womenfolk, their slaves, such men as attend them who have no sexual desire, or children who are not yet aware of women's nakedness; they should not stamp their feet so as to draw attention to any hidden charms. Believers, all of you, turn to God so that you may prosper.

(*al- Nur* 24:31)

This is the dress code. Islam is a religion that teaches us every aspect of our life. Islam can be called a *deen* of prevention. It is not a *deen* of treatment. Treatment comes later on, after we fail to take preventative steps and precautions. So what is the prevention to keep morality in communities? Morality on this Earth requires measures and guidance in the interaction between the two genders. A part of maintaining morality is in how both genders interact and how women dress. If we want to keep this Earth that Allah ﷻ made us representatives of, beautiful, then our conduct on His Earth should be in a way that pleases Him.

May Allah ﷻ make it easy for all of us to understand and put His guidance into practise. Ya Rabbi Amīn.

Points to reflect on:

- Clothing is a blessing from Allah ﷻ and is linked in the Qur'an to how we conduct ourselves.
- The standard for all men and women is to interact with respect and avoid looking inappropriately at each other.
- Modesty, *Hayah* is a virtue and praiseworthy. If we are modest in our behaviour and what we wear, it has a positive impact on our community.

- It is natural to want to wear good clothes that suit us, the Qur'an confirms this. We need to make sure we observe the guidelines when we focus on our appearance.

- The metaphor of *taqwa* – God consciousness – being the best garment tells us where our focus should be when we think about our appearance.

يَـٰبَنِىٓ ءَادَمَ خُذُوا۟ زِينَتَكُمْ عِندَ كُلِّ مَسْجِدٍ وَكُلُوا۟ وَٱشْرَبُوا۟ وَلَا تُسْرِفُوٓا۟ ۚ إِنَّهُۥ لَا
يُحِبُّ ٱلْمُسْرِفِينَ ۝

Children of Adam, dress well whenever you are at worship, and eat and drink [as We have permitted] but do not be extravagant: God does not like extravagant people.

(*al-Aʿrāf* 7:31)

Chapter 16

WHAT DOES THE QUR'AN SAY ABOUT SOCIAL RELATIONS?

When Allah ﷻ put us on this Earth as a community, did He give us rules or guidelines for how we conduct ourselves? The answer is yes. The chapter in the Qur'an called *Al Hujurat*-The Rooms, or The Compartments, is also known as the 'chapter of conduct' and should be known to everybody.

Being Misunderstood

All of us have felt the pain and hurt when someone has ill feelings towards them. We might think or say 'I didn't do it, I didn't say it for that reason', but someone took our comment or actions negatively. The painful feelings are even worse when we learn that someone talked about us in a negative way.

What did Allah ﷻ say about this?

يَـٰٓأَيُّهَا ٱلَّذِينَ ءَامَنُوا۟ ٱجْتَنِبُوا۟ كَثِيرًا مِّنَ ٱلظَّنِّ إِنَّ بَعْضَ ٱلظَّنِّ إِثْمٌ ۖ وَلَا تَجَسَّسُوا۟
وَلَا يَغْتَب بَّعْضُكُم بَعْضًا ۚ أَيُحِبُّ أَحَدُكُمْ أَن يَأْكُلَ لَحْمَ أَخِيهِ مَيْتًا فَكَرِهْتُمُوهُ ۚ
وَٱتَّقُوا۟ ٱللَّهَ ۚ إِنَّ ٱللَّهَ تَوَّابٌ رَّحِيمٌ ۝

'O Believers, avoid making too many assumptions- some (suspicions) assumptions are sinful- and do not spy on one another or speak ill of people behind their backs: would any of you like to eat the flesh of your dead brother? No, you would hate it. So be mindful of God: God is ever relenting, most merciful.'

(*al-Hujurat* 49:12)

Every time we read or hear these words in the Qur'an يَـٰٓأَيُّهَا ٱلَّذِينَ ءَامَنُو 'O believers', or 'O you who believe', we need to give our full attention and understand what Allah ﷻ wants from you and I.

The first order is: stay away from suspicion. Then we are told don't feel or think ill of somebody else, as some of this suspicion is actually a sin. Next we are told: do not backbite each other, and Allah ﷻ then asks us a rhetorical question to which we have no answer:

أَيُحِبُّ أَحَدُكُمْ أَن يَأْكُلَ لَحْمَ أَخِيهِ مَيْتًا ۝

Do you really want to eat the flesh of your dead brother?

Finally this *ayah* reminds us to be conscious of Allah ﷻ as He always accepts repentance, and He is All Merciful. In this way the Qur'an addresses the subject of moral conduct by including our feelings and these feelings are shaped by how we behave with each other. The Qur'an brings focus on our behaviour with everyone, urging us to reflect: how should I behave towards another person and vice versa? We have to guarantee that every human being, Muslim and non-Muslims' rights are respected with integrity and that we value their presence.

Avoid suspicion and backbiting

Allah ﷻ, specifically named two things to avoid: suspicion and backbiting, which *Rasul Allah* ﷺ also taught us about. When asked what to do if we suspect someone is doing something, but we don't have proof, he ﷺ replied إذَا ظَنَنْتَ فَلَا تحَقَّق, if you have the feeling of suspicion, don't تحَقَّق, investigate, don't interrogate, just leave it. If it's true, Allah ﷻ will show you and will bring the reality in front of you. We are also warned not to spy in the same verse.

In today's context, that includes not picking up somebody's phone to see what they are saying in their text messages. When we respect that all human beings have rights, we wouldn't want to disrespect them by spying.

The important subject of backbiting is next in this verse: وَلَا يَغْتَبْ بَعْضُكُمْ بَعْضًا. What is the definition of backbiting? ذِكْرُ أَخِيكَ بِمَا يَكْرَه إذَا بَلَغَه. It is explained by *Rasul Allah* ﷺ in this hadith:

> Abu Hurayrah ؓ narrated that the Messenger of Allah ﷺ said: "Do you know what *ghibah* (backbiting) is?" They said, "Allah and His Messenger know best." He said, "Saying something about your brother that he dislikes." It was asked, "What if what I say about my brother is true?" He said, "If what you say is true then you have backbitten about him, and if it is not true, then you have slandered (*buhtan*) him."
>
> [Muslim].

The punishment for slander *buhtan* is detailed in the Qur'an.

Anytime we come across vivid imagery in a metaphor or simile in the Qur'an, this means Allah ﷻ wants to bring our attention to a phenomenon that is either going to make it clearer, or is going to make it more beloved or disliked, as the context requires.

The rhetorical question, *do you really want to eat the flesh of your brother?* Has an immediate reply from Allah ﷻ when He says, فَكَرِهْتُمُوهُ, 'you don't like it.' Who would want to do that? When *Rasul Allah* ﷺ was coming back from a graveyard after a burial, he heard two people behind him, saying something negative about the dead person. As he was walking, there was a dead animal on the side of the road. He looked at them and told them to go and eat from it. And they said, 'Ya *Rasul Allah*, how can we eat from it? And his ﷺ reply was: 'You already did'.

***Taqwa*-the cure**

Today backbiting has become so common between everybody, that it is normalised. *Shaytan* even influences us to justify it and feel that we haven't said anything which is wrong. You may be thinking how can we not do something which unfortunately has now become so common? Allah ﷻ gives us an antidote, or medicine to cure us when He says: وَٱتَّقُوا۟ ٱللَّهَ be Allah conscious – this is one remedy. If these thoughts come to us, we need to remind ourselves that Allah ﷻ is hearing us and watching us, which should discourage this behaviour.

A second remedy comes from applying the hadith of *Rasul Allah* ﷺ

يُؤْمِنُ أَحَدُكُمْ حَتَّى يُحِبَّ لأَخِيهِ مَا يُحِبُّ لِنَفْسِهِ

On the authority of Abu Hamzah, Anas bin Malik ﷺ reported that the Prophet ﷺ said: None of you [truly] believes until he loves for his brother that which he loves for himself. (Bukhari)

By standing in our brother or sister's shoes, we can question our own re-action before we speak; *would I be happy if someone said this about me?* The answer will be no, so the remedy we come back to is: وَٱتَّقُوا۟ ٱللَّهَ: Be conscious of Allah ﷻ, and in this context we should hold our tongue out of fear of Allah ﷻ. *Rasul Allah* ﷺ also taught us,

مَنْ كَانَ يُؤْمِنُ بِاللَّهِ وَالْيَوْمِ الآخِرِ فَلْيَقُلْ خَيْرًا أَوْ لِيَصْمُتْ

"He who believes in Allah ﷻ and the Last Day must either speak good or remain silent."

We can ask ourselves: *do I do this, or at least aim do this? Am I conscious that Allah ﷻ knows everything I said?*

At the end of the verse, إِنَّ ٱللَّهَ تَوَّابٌ الرَّحِيمٌ. Allah ﷻ reassures us that He accepts repentance and we can ask Allah ﷻ for forgiveness when we fall short, as He is Merciful.

If we make this mistake and realise, we should make *du'a* for that person. If we don't remember who we spoke about, we can say 'Ya Allah, please forgive everybody that I have backbitten and everybody I said something negative about.'

The beauty of Islam is that it not only raises difficult issues to the surface, but it brings with it a treatment. So let's all make a promise to ourselves, to ask Allah ﷻ to make it easy for us to control our tongue and ask Allah ﷻ for us to say what is good and pleasing to Allah ﷻ. Ya Rabbi Amīn.

Points to reflect on:

- Suspicion is the one type of thought that can be a sin and we don't realise it. So we need to be extra cautious about allowing assumptions to enter our minds.
- Every person deserves privacy and dignity and we can uphold this in homes, workplaces and social circles. Prying in matters that don't concern us, or spying on people damages trust.
- Our words have consequences, in particular if they are behind someone's back. Always check: would I want this said about me?
- *Tawqa* – God consciousness is the best prevention against suspicion and backbiting.
- Remembering that the etiquettes of interacting with one another are part of our *deen*, should help us to be mindful of this at all times.

يَـٰٓأَيُّهَا ٱلَّذِينَ ءَامَنُوا۟ لَا يَسْخَرْ قَوْمٌ مِّن قَوْمٍ عَسَىٰٓ أَن يَكُونُوا۟ خَيْرًا مِّنْهُمْ وَلَا
نِسَآءٌ مِّن نِّسَآءٍ عَسَىٰٓ أَن يَكُنَّ خَيْرًا مِّنْهُنَّ ۖ وَلَا تَلْمِزُوٓا۟ أَنفُسَكُمْ
وَلَا تَنَابَزُوا۟ بِٱلْأَلْقَـٰبِ ۖ بِئْسَ ٱلِٱسْمُ ٱلْفُسُوقُ بَعْدَ ٱلْإِيمَـٰنِ ۚ وَمَن لَّمْ
يَتُبْ فَأُو۟لَـٰٓئِكَ هُمُ ٱلظَّـٰلِمُونَ ﴿١١﴾

Believers, no one group of men should jeer at another, who may after all be better than them; no one group of women should jeer at another, who may after all be better than them; do not speak ill of one another; do not use offensive nicknames for one another. How bad it is to be called a mischief-maker after accepting faith! Those who do not repent of this behaviour are evildoers.

(*al-Hujurat* 49:11)

Chapter 17

THIS LIFE

What does the Qur'an say about this life?

In Chapter four we explored the main purpose Allah ﷻ created us for; to worship Him alone and be His representative on Earth. Our period of time here is limited; some of us have many years, some have less, before moving on to the afterlife. It is natural that we have many questions and wonder about what the Qur'an says about our worldly life. What does Allah ﷻ say? He gives us guidance in various contexts and the first one we'll look at is in *Surah Yunus*. Allah ﷻ says:

إِنَّمَا مَثَلُ الْحَيَاةِ الدُّنْيَا كَمَاءٍ أَنْزَلْنَاهُ مِنَ السَّمَاءِ فَاخْتَلَطَ بِهِ نَبَاتُ الْأَرْضِ مِمَّا
يَأْكُلُ النَّاسُ وَالْأَنْعَامُ حَتَّىٰ إِذَا أَخَذَتِ الْأَرْضُ زُخْرُفَهَا وَازَّيَّنَتْ وَظَنَّ أَهْلُهَا أَنَّهُمْ
قَادِرُونَ عَلَيْهَا أَتَاهَا أَمْرُنَا لَيْلًا أَوْ نَهَارًا فَجَعَلْنَاهَا حَصِيدًا كَأَنْ لَمْ تَغْنَ بِالْأَمْسِ

The life of this world is like this: rain that We send down from the sky is absorbed by the plants of the Earth, from which humans and animals eat. But when the Earth has taken on its finest appearance, and adorns itself, and its people think they have power over it, then the fate We commanded comes to it, by night or by day, and We reduce it to stubble, as if it had not flourished just the day before. This is the way We explain the revelations for those who reflect.

(*Yunus* 10:24)

The Parable of this life

There are several parables in the Qur'an which use our imagination to teach particular lessons. Allah ﷻ is giving a parable here from something we experience quite regularly in this *dunya*. In this *ayah*, this worldly life-cycle you and I are living is compared to the cycle of water and nature. When rain is sent down from the sky, it is absorbed by the Earth and plants. This allows crops to grow which then feeds mankind and livestock.

The parable shares the scene of how the Earth possesses beauty and adornment, and when people see it they believe they have complete control over these resources. Then Allah ﷻ tells us when His command comes either by night or the day, the harvest can disappear, as though nothing had previously flourished. Allah ﷻ is telling us that He gives signs for the people who think, reflect and see.

Nature's cycle and the human life-cycle

What is Allah ﷻ telling us here? He is showing us through this parable, the true reality of this world. The rainfall is symbolic of the stage of our birth. The image of rain producing fruits, vegetation and plants which people and animals eat from, mirrors our youth and growing in strength. As we continue with this life, and become adults, we study, work and experience success in different areas of life, like careers, having our own family and our children. We reach a stage where we have everything we want, and we believe we have everything under control.

Then Allah ﷻ says when people reach this stage of contentment and strength to control their affairs, أَتَىٰهَآ أَمْرُنَا. the commands of Allah ﷻ suddenly come during the day or night. And through His commands, everything can become ashes and disappear into nothing. We see this all the time in our daily lives. Somebody, for example was very successful and then he or she gets sick and they cannot function anymore. Or, someone was very wealthy with investments and suddenly the stock market crashes and they lose everything. Or, tragically a car accident takes place and a family is shattered. May Allah ﷻ protect everybody, especially everyone's families. Amīn.

The most important thing that Allah ﷻ is telling us is that at one point in this worldly life, we will leave everything behind, and this world will cease to exist: كَأَن لَّمْ تَغْنَ بِٱلْأَمْسِ. As though the beautiful yesterdays were never here. The mindset, you and I need to live with, is the following: we are here, but we are not here forever. We are here to enjoy this beautiful world, but we are not here *only* to enjoy. There is much more to discover about what Allah ﷻ wants us to understand about this *dunya*, where we spend all our time. The following chapter will continue with this journey to discover more answers about this world from the Qur'an.

Points to reflect on:

- Life is like the growth of vegetation after rain, full of hope and beauty. Yet we are reminded this growth is temporary. When we appreciate this it helps us value the gift of life.

- When we experience sudden changes like loss or illness, it reminds us that it is Our Creator who is in control and we put our trust in Him.

- The parable of the Earth's cycle reminds us of the cycle of our lives, from birth to decline. Reflecting on this helps us to be grounded and use our time with wisdom for our hereafter.

- Everything in this world belongs to Allah ﷻ, even when we feel most in control. Remembering this makes us grateful for all our blessings.

أَفَمَن يَعْلَمُ أَنَّمَآ أُنزِلَ إِلَيْكَ مِن رَّبِّكَ ٱلْحَقُّ كَمَنْ هُوَ أَعْمَىٰٓ ۚ إِنَّمَا يَتَذَكَّرُ أُو۟لُوا۟
ٱلْأَلْبَٰبِ ۝ ٱلَّذِينَ يُوفُونَ بِعَهْدِ ٱللَّهِ وَلَا يَنقُضُونَ ٱلْمِيثَٰقَ ۝ وَٱلَّذِينَ يَصِلُونَ مَآ
أَمَرَ ٱللَّهُ بِهِۦٓ أَن يُوصَلَ وَيَخْشَوْنَ رَبَّهُمْ وَيَخَافُونَ سُوٓءَ ٱلْحِسَابِ ۝ وَٱلَّذِينَ
صَبَرُوا۟ ٱبْتِغَآءَ وَجْهِ رَبِّهِمْ وَأَقَامُوا۟ ٱلصَّلَوٰةَ وَأَنفَقُوا۟ مِمَّا رَزَقْنَٰهُمْ سِرًّا وَعَلَانِيَةً
وَيَدْرَءُونَ بِٱلْحَسَنَةِ ٱلسَّيِّئَةَ أُو۟لَٰٓئِكَ لَهُمْ عُقْبَى ٱلدَّارِ ۝ جَنَّٰتُ عَدْنٍ يَدْخُلُونَهَا
وَمَن صَلَحَ مِنْ ءَابَآئِهِمْ وَأَزْوَٰجِهِمْ وَذُرِّيَّٰتِهِمْ ۖ وَٱلْمَلَٰٓئِكَةُ يَدْخُلُونَ عَلَيْهِم مِّن كُلِّ
بَابٍ ۝ سَلَٰمٌ عَلَيْكُم بِمَا صَبَرْتُمْ ۚ فَنِعْمَ عُقْبَى ٱلدَّارِ ۝ وَٱلَّذِينَ يَنقُضُونَ عَهْدَ
ٱللَّهِ مِنۢ بَعْدِ مِيثَٰقِهِۦ وَيَقْطَعُونَ مَآ أَمَرَ ٱللَّهُ بِهِۦٓ أَن يُوصَلَ وَيُفْسِدُونَ فِى
ٱلْأَرْضِ ۙ أُو۟لَٰٓئِكَ لَهُمُ ٱللَّعْنَةُ وَلَهُمْ سُوٓءُ ٱلدَّارِ ۝ ٱللَّهُ يَبْسُطُ ٱلرِّزْقَ لِمَن يَشَآءُ
وَيَقْدِرُ ۚ وَفَرِحُوا۟ بِٱلْحَيَوٰةِ ٱلدُّنْيَا وَمَا ٱلْحَيَوٰةُ ٱلدُّنْيَا فِى ٱلْءَاخِرَةِ إِلَّا مَتَٰعٌ

Is someone who knows that what was revealed to you from your Lord is the truth, be like someone who is blind? Only those who possess intellect reflect. Those who fulfil the promise to Allah, and do not violate the agreement. And those who join what Allah has commanded to be joined, and fear their Lord, and dread the dire reckoning. And those who patiently seek their Lord's attention, and pray regularly, and donate from what We have provided for them—secretly and openly—and repel evil with good. For them, there is the Ultimate Home. Everlasting Gardens, which they will enter, along with the righteous from among their parents, and their spouses, and their descendants. And the angels will enter upon them from every gate. "Peace be upon you—because you were patient. How excellent is the Final Home." As for those who violate the promise to Allah, after pledging to keep it, and sever what Allah has commanded to be joined, and work corruption on Earth: it is they who will have the curse, and theirs is the Worst Home. Allah dispenses the sustenance to whomever He wills—and restricts. And they delight in the worldly life. Yet the worldly life, compared to the Hereafter, is nothing but enjoyment.

(*al-Ra'd* 13:19-26)

Chapter 18

WHAT DOES THE QUR'AN SAY ABOUT LIVING A BALANCED LIFE?

This chapter continues with what the Qur'an tells us about life in this *dunya*. When we contemplate on the verses about this life, we find that Allah ﷻ teaches us through certain concepts; what people desire; in comparison to the hereafter and centering *taqwa* – God consciousness. Let's look at these in more detail.

What people desire in this life

زُيِّنَ لِلنَّاسِ حُبُّ الشَّهَوَاتِ مِنَ النِّسَاءِ وَالْبَنِينَ وَالْقَنَاطِيرِ الْمُقَنطَرَةِ
مِنَ الذَّهَبِ وَالْفِضَّةِ وَالْخَيْلِ الْمُسَوَّمَةِ وَالْأَنْعَامِ وَالْحَرْثِ ۗ ذَٰلِكَ
مَتَاعُ الْحَيَاةِ الدُّنْيَا ۖ وَاللَّهُ عِندَهُ حُسْنُ الْمَآبِ

Adorned for people is the love of desires: women, and children, and piles upon piles of gold and silver, and branded horses, and livestock, and fields. These are the conveniences of the worldly life, while with Allah is the best place to return.

(*al-Imran* 3:14)

When we read the Qur'an and reflect on it, we face the fact that worldly desires زُيِّنَ لِلنَّاسِ have been made beautiful to people. Then, Allah ﷻ explains which desires people love; حُبُّ ٱلشَّهَوَٰتِ مِنَ ٱلنِّسَآءِ, for the man, it is women and then comes the love of children, gold and silver, وَٱلْخَيْلِ ٱلْمُسَوَّمَةِ. and a certain kind of horse that has a special mark on the forehead. The contemporary equivalent to coveted horses would be expensive cars, وَٱلْخَيْلِ ٱلْمُسَوَّمَةِ وَٱلْأَنْعَٰمِ وَٱلْحَرْثِ. The love of livestock signifies beyond animals, any type of wealth such as businesses, and finally the love of owning land, which is another desire people chase in this world.

Allah ﷻ doesn't say any of these desires are bad, and doesn't rebuke us for loving these, or question why we love these. He enumerates these permissible things and said, ذَٰلِكَ مَتَٰعُ ٱلْحَيَوٰةِ ٱلدُّنْيَا that this is the enjoyment of this life. In the previous chapter when we looked at the verses from *Surah Yunus* about our life cycle from birth to adulthood, we were reminded that in adulthood we are attracted to all this beauty and want to enjoy life; this *ayah* of *Surah al-Imran* lists what we enjoy. Then, Allah ﷻ reminds us of something else; that while these are the conveniences of life, what is with Allah ﷻ is the better place we will return to.

A superior focus

In the following verse, Allah ﷻ asks:

قُلْ أَؤُنَبِّئُكُم بِخَيْرٍ مِّن ذَٰلِكُمْ ۞

Would you like me to tell you of things that are better than all of these?
(*al-Imran* 3:15)

Then He sets out what is better than the desires of the worldly life:

لِلَّذِينَ ٱتَّقَوْا۟ عِندَ رَبِّهِمْ جَنَّـٰتٌ تَجْرِى مِن تَحْتِهَا ٱلْأَنْهَـٰرُ خَـٰلِدِينَ فِيهَا وَأَزْوَٰجٌ مُّطَهَّرَةٌ وَرِضْوَٰنٌ مِّنَ ٱللَّهِ ۗ وَٱللَّهُ بَصِيرٌۢ بِٱلْعِبَادِ ۞

Their Lord will give those who are mindful of God, Gardens graced with flowing streams, where they will stay with pure spouses and God's good pleasure- God is fully aware of His servants.
(*al-Imran* 3:15)

The God-conscious one

The promise of what is better than this life's attractions is addressed specifically to the people of *taqwa*, to those people who are conscious of Allah ﷻ. One may question what does a God conscious person get from our Rabb? جَنَّـٰتٌ تَجْرِى مِن تَحْتِهَا ٱلْأَنْهَـٰرُ خَـٰلِدِينَ فِيهَا. *You will get gardens to dwell in eternally with rivers that flow beneath them*, with pure spouses. In addition to all these material things, we will gain the pleasure of Allah ﷻ. At the end of this verse we are reminded:

وَٱللَّهُ بَصِيرٌۢ بِٱلْعِبَادِ

And Allah is well aware of what human beings do

ٱلَّذِينَ يَقُولُونَ رَبَّنَآ إِنَّنَآ ءَامَنَّا فَٱغْفِرْ لَنَا ذُنُوبَنَا وَقِنَا عَذَابَ ٱلنَّارِ

those who say, "Our Lord, we believe, so forgive us our sins and protect us from suffering in the Fire,"

ٱلصَّـٰبِرِينَ وَٱلصَّـٰدِقِينَ وَٱلْقَـٰنِتِينَ وَٱلْمُنفِقِينَ وَٱلْمُسْتَغْفِرِينَ بِٱلْأَسْحَارِ

those who are steadfast, truthful, truly devout, who give [in God's cause] and pray before dawn for forgiveness.'
(*al-Imran* 3:16-17)

Here, reality is described. We love what is in the *dunya* but there is something better for those who remain conscious of God, who are truthful and devout in their worship.

So we see there are many verses in the Qur'an that answer our questions about this worldly life. The next *ayah* we will reflect on, is the verse of *Surah al-Hadid*, which combines the following two points. The verse starts with اعلموا, which we need to take note of. Every time Allah ﷻ says اعلموا, it literally means 'pay attention' meaning it is something we should know. The verse starts drawing our attention to a fact, انما, meaning something definite:

ٱعْلَمُوٓا۟ أَنَّمَا ٱلْحَيَوٰةُ ٱلدُّنْيَا لَعِبٌ وَلَهْوٌ وَزِينَةٌ وَتَفَاخُرٌۢ بَيْنَكُمْ وَتَكَاثُرٌ فِى ٱلْأَمْوَٰلِ وَٱلْأَوْلَـٰدِ ۖ كَمَثَلِ غَيْثٍ أَعْجَبَ ٱلْكُفَّارَ نَبَاتُهُۥ ثُمَّ يَهِيجُ فَتَرَىٰهُ مُصْفَرًّا ثُمَّ يَكُونُ حُطَـٰمًا ۖ وَفِى ٱلْـَٔاخِرَةِ عَذَابٌ شَدِيدٌ وَمَغْفِرَةٌ مِّنَ ٱللَّهِ وَرِضْوَٰنٌ ۚ وَمَا ٱلْحَيَوٰةُ ٱلدُّنْيَآ إِلَّا مَتَـٰعُ ٱلْغُرُورِ ۝

Bear in mind that the present life is just a game, a diversion, an attraction, a cause of boasting among you, of rivalry in wealth and children. It is like plants that spring up after the rain: their growth at first delights the sowers, but then you see them wither away, turn yellow, and become stubble. There is terrible punishment in the next life as well as forgiveness and approval from God; the life of this world is only an illusory pleasure.

(*al-Hadid* 57:20)

Here, Allah ﷻ has combined several elements, so let's consider them in detail. We can ask ourselves some questions such as 'What is this daily hectic life, the business and juggling multiple things that we keep ourselves busy with?' لَعِبٌ وَلَهْوٌ. We are told it is play and amusement, distraction and competition between people. But this is how life is, so how do we remind ourselves of its transience? We need to look at cycles in nature which is why Allah ﷻ always gives us examples. كَمَثَلِ غَيْثٍ أَعْجَبَ ٱلْكُفَّارَ نَبَاتُهُۥ. When it rains, it's a reminder when we're outdoors, or gardening, to look, really look and remember this verse about the true position of this life.

When we plant seeds or a small plant, and water it and give it time to grow, we witness how it becomes a beautiful flower or a huge tree. But how long will this last? And then what happens? ثُمَّ يَهِيجُ فَتَرَىٰهُ مُصْفَرًّا In the same way, as plants and trees, we get old and weak and then we die. And then what's waiting for us there? ٱلْـَٔاخِرَةِ عَذَابٌ شَدِيدٌ وَمَغْفِرَةٌ مِّنَ ٱللَّهِ وَرِضْوَٰنٌ-W have two choices. Either it's going to be severe punishment or it is going to be forgiveness from Allah ﷻ. It all depends on what we did here. What did we do with all that He gave us? The beauty, the children, the wealth, the job; in the end, there are these two results and our place in the hereafter depends on what we chose in this *dunya.*

We can ask ourselves and reflect: did I choose whatever Allah ﷻ gave me from the wealth, the children, the money, the status, to work for my *akhirah* more than for the *dunya?* If I've worked for my *akhirah* then forgiveness and the pleasure of Allah ﷻ is waiting for me. The opposite faces us too: if I am going to spend my time focusing on beauty, career, children and competing to be the best without any thought of the *akhirah,* then Allah ﷻ may give what I'm after in the *dunya.* But if I disobey His limits and ignore His guidance, then am I heading towards severe punishment?

Allah ﷻ teaches us this important concept. Many of these concepts help us to live this life in balance. We want to live in this *dunya* the way it pleases Allah ﷻ and enjoy what He gave us, but at the same time, we never want to get distracted from our eternal destination. May Allah ﷻ protect us all.

Points to reflect on:

- Allah ﷻ is teaching us about the real focus in life which is gaining His pleasure through *taqwa* – God consciousness.
- We need to evaluate our attachment to the things we love in this world, to keep balance.
- We should focus on the *akhirah* with our goals, and prioritise what is significant over trivia.
- Remind ourselves that Allah ﷻ has the ultimate authority to reward, punish, forgive and hold us to account for what we choose to do in this life.
- Ponder on how we can use the blessings we receive to benefit our hereafter.
- Check our intentions are solely for Allah ﷻ. If we do things to please people, they could become a source of test for us, even if they are our nearest family and dearest possessions.

وَٱعْلَمُوٓا۟ أَنَّمَآ أَمْوَٰلُكُمْ وَأَوْلَٰدُكُمْ فِتْنَةٌ وَأَنَّ ٱللَّهَ عِندَهُۥٓ أَجْرٌ عَظِيمٌ

"And know that your properties and your children are but a trial and that Allāh has with Him a great reward."

(*al-Anfal* 8:28)

Chapter 19

WHAT DOES THE QUR'AN SAY ABOUT MONEY?

A huge part of this life is about earning and using money. For both men and women, this resource of money can come in multiple ways to help us, or become a source of stress and problems. Is this subject that affects us all in one way or another mentioned in the Qur'an. Did Allah ﷻ speak about money? The answer is yes and it is mentioned in different contexts. This verse of *Surah al-Kahf* puts money in the context of the adornments of this life:

ٱلْمَالُ وَٱلْبَنُونَ زِينَةُ ٱلْحَيَوٰةِ ٱلدُّنْيَا ۖ

Wealth and children are the attractions of this worldly life, but

وَٱلْبَـٰقِيَـٰتُ ٱلصَّـٰلِحَـٰتُ خَيْرٌ عِندَ رَبِّكَ ثَوَابًا وَخَيْرٌ أَمَلًا

lasting righteous deeds have a better reward with your Lord and give better grounds for hope.

(*al-Kahf* 18:46)

Scholars are of the opinion that 'lasting righteous deeds' is a reference to the *dhikr* of Allah ﷻ:

سُبْحَانَ اللّهِ وَالْحَمْدُ لِلّهِ وَلاَ إِلَهَ إِلاَّ اللّهُ وَاللّهُ أَكْبَرُ وَلاَ حَوْلَ وَلاَ قُوَّةَ إِلاَّ بِاللّٰه

"Glory be to Allah, and all praise is for Allah, and there is no god but Allah, and Allah is the Greatest. There is no power and no strength except with Allah."

So the first context we find is that Allah ﷻ mentioned wealth here as the beauty of the *dunya*.

The example of Qarun

If we look at *Surah al-Qasas* where Allah ﷻ talks about money and how wealthy people should behave concerning their wealth. Allah ﷻ gives us the example of Qarun who was from the people of Musa, yet he transgressed against them and Allah ﷻ shows us exactly what He did. The story starts:

إِنَّ قَـٰرُونَ كَانَ مِن قَوْمِ مُوسَىٰ فَبَغَىٰ عَلَيْهِمْ

Qarun belonged to the people of Moses, but he exploited them.

(*al-Qasas* 28:76)

Allah ﷻ didn't specify how much his wealth was, but He gives us a clue: just the keys for the treasures would be very difficult for a group of strong men to carry.

وَآتَيْنَاهُ مِنَ الْكُنُوزِ مَا إِنَّ مَفَاتِحَهُ لَتَنُوءُ بِالْعُصْبَةِ أُولِي الْقُوَّةِ

We had given him treasures, the keys of which would burden a group of strong men.

(*al-Qasas* 28:76)

So we can imagine how much wealth he had. You may think, there is nothing that's wrong with that, some people *are* wealthy. The problem was in his attitude and thinking.

قَالَ لَهُۥ قَوْمُهُۥ لَا تَفْرَحْ ۖ إِنَّ ٱللَّهَ لَا يُحِبُّ ٱلْفَرِحِينَ

His people told him not to be too arrogant, Allah doesn't love those who are exultant.

What his people warned him about was the feeling of pride and arrogance, showing off or feeling they are better than other people. You may think if Allah ﷻ gave someone some money, shouldn't they spend it? Allah ﷻ responds to our thoughts as He knows what we think, hence the people of Qarun continued to counsel him:

وَابْتَغِ فِيمَا آتَاكَ اللَّهُ الدَّارَ الْآخِرَةَ ۖ وَلَا تَنسَ نَصِيبَكَ مِنَ الدُّنْيَا
وَأَحْسِن كَمَا أَحْسَنَ اللَّهُ إِلَيْكَ

But seek, with what Allah has given you, the Home of the Hereafter. And do not neglect your share of this world. And be charitable, as Allah is charitable to you.

(*al-Qasas* 28:77)

The advice hones in on the main focus of spending our money is to use it for our *akhirah* to achieve a higher station with the money Allah ﷻ gave us. At the same time this does not mean that we live in a state of poverty when Allah ﷻ has blessed us with wealth, as our *deen* teaches us balance.

وَلَا تَنسَ نَصِيبَكَ مِنَ ٱلدُّنْيَا ۖ وَأَحْسِن كَمَآ أَحْسَنَ ٱللَّهُ إِلَيْكَ ۖ

(*al-Qasas* 28:77)

The people are reminding him to do good, to excel and be kind in your conduct, just as Allah ﷻ was kind and generous to you. Crucially, they remind Qarun that the money was not from him, Allah ﷻ gave it to him. Then they warned him and gave the reason why:

وَأَحْسِن كَمَآ أَحْسَنَ ٱللَّهُ إِلَيْكَ ۖ وَلَا تَبْغِ ٱلْفَسَادَ فِى ٱلْأَرْضِ ۖ

Do not use the wealth that Allah gave you to spread mischief on this Earth

(*al-Qasas* 28:77)

because

إِنَّ ٱللَّهَ لَا يُحِبُّ ٱلْمُفْسِدِينَ.

Allah does not love those who spread corruption and mischief.

(*al-Qasas* 28:77)

They gave him advice without expecting anything from him. Let's look at Qarun's response:

قَالَ إِنَّمَآ أُوتِيتُهُۥ عَلَىٰ عِلْمٍ عِندِىٓ ۚ

He said "I was able to obtain this because of the knowledge I have".

(*al-Qasas* 28:78)

In other words, he said I deserve this wealth because of my expertise and knowledge, I worked hard for it; I am smart. It is all my effort that has led to everything that I have. The same verse continues with Allah's ﷻ caution:

أَوَلَمْ يَعْلَمْ أَنَّ ٱللَّهَ قَدْ أَهْلَكَ مِن قَبْلِهِۦ مِنَ ٱلْقُرُونِ مَنْ هُوَ أَشَدُّ مِنْهُ قُوَّةً وَأَكْثَرُ
جَمْعًا ۚ وَلَا يُسْـَٔلُ عَن ذُنُوبِهِمُ ٱلْمُجْرِمُونَ.

Didn't he realise that Allah destroyed people of previous generations who were far stronger and wealthier than him? The guilty won't be asked about their sins.

(*al-Qasas* 28:78)

Allah ﷻ responds here and reminds him that previous nations had far more riches than him and were destroyed. After they sinned, they were not given a second chance.

Now, with this advice, what did he do? He continued in the same vein, nothing changed. In this is a lesson for us too; money usually corrupts people as stated in *Surah Yusuf* 'إِلَّا مَا رَحِمَ رَبِّهِ', '*Except those on whom my Lord has mercy*' (*Yusuf* 12:53). The narrative continues in the following verse:

فَخَرَجَ عَلَىٰ قَوْمِهِۦ فِى زِينَتِهِۦ ۖ
قَالَ ٱلَّذِينَ يُرِيدُونَ ٱلْحَيَوٰةَ ٱلدُّنْيَا.
يَـٰلَيْتَ لَنَا مِثْلَ مَآ أُوتِىَ قَـٰرُونُ إِنَّهُۥ لَذُو حَظٍّ عَظِيمٍ.

So he went out among his people in his adornment. Those who desired the worldly life said, "Oh would that we had like what was given to Qarun. Indeed he is one of great fortune."

(*al-Qasas* 28:79)

We are not told how he went out amongst his people, but he appeared before them with his wealth, which was attractive to his people who thought him to be fortunate. We see this around us too, when people see others with more than them – he has this car, he has this house, she has that jewellery, and then one longs for the same. However, the next *ayah* shows a contrast from the people with beneficial knowledge who say something else-we witness their dialogue:

وَقَالَ ٱلَّذِينَ أُوتُوا۟ ٱلْعِلْمَ.

Those who have knowledge, say, " وَيْلَكُمْ, *woe on you!*

ثَوَابُ ٱللَّهِ خَيْرٌ لِّمَنْ ءَامَنَ وَعَمِلَ صَـٰلِحًا وَلَا يُلَقَّىٰهَآ إِلَّا ٱلصَّـٰبِرُونَ.

Allah's rewards for believers and the righteous is better; the patient will achieve that."

(*al-Qasas* 28:80)

People of beneficial knowledge could see that this wealth and glamour was temporary. They knew that this will not give them what Allah ﷻ wants for them in the *akhirah*. The rewards of Allah ﷻ are way more than the worldly material things. Who is going to get the reward of Allah? It is those who believe, وَعَمِلَ صَالِحًا and do good deeds and are patient. This is why Allah ﷻ said, *righteousness is better, the patient will achieve that*. Why is patience mentioned here? Those who are patient are not lured by the *dunya*, and don't get corrupted by wealth or become jealous when they don't have what other people have.

What happened next? As Qarun walked arrogantly, the punishment fell on him immediately which Allah ﷻ sent:

فَخَسَفْنَا بِهِۦ وَبِدَارِهِ ٱلْأَرْضَ
فَمَا كَانَ لَهُۥ مِن فِئَةٍ يَنصُرُونَهُۥ مِن دُونِ ٱللَّهِ وَمَا كَانَ مِنَ ٱلْمُنتَصِرِينَ.

We made the Earth swallow him and his house. There was no rescue party to help him beside Allah, nor was he able to protect himself.

(*al-Qasas* 28:81)

وَأَصْبَحَ ٱلَّذِينَ تَمَنَّوْا۟ مَكَانَهُۥ بِٱلْأَمْسِ يَقُولُونَ وَيْكَأَنَّ ٱللَّهَ يَبْسُطُ ٱلرِّزْقَ لِمَن يَشَآءُ مِنْ عِبَادِهِۦ وَيَقْدِرُ ۖ لَوْلَآ أَن مَّنَّ ٱللَّهُ عَلَيْنَا لَخَسَفَ بِنَا ۖ وَيْكَأَنَّهُۥ لَا يُفْلِحُ ٱلْكَٰفِرُونَ

The next day, those who had, the day before, wished to be in his place exclaimed, 'Alas [for you, Qarun]! It is God alone who gives what He wills, abundantly or sparingly, to whichever He wills of His creatures: if God had not been gracious to us, He would have caused the Earth to swallow us too.' Alas indeed! Those who are ungrateful will never prosper.

(*al-Qasas* 28:82)

Those people who had envied Qarun were now saying after seeing what happened, that it is indeed Allah's ﷻ choice to give to whom He chooses or to withhold. The reminder at the end of this verse is for us all:

وَيْكَأَنَّهُۥ لَا يُفْلِحُ ٱلْكَٰفِرُونَ.

Those who are ungrateful will never be successful.

What do we learn from this powerful story and advice?

Firstly, money and wealth come from Allah ﷻ. Even if we work very hard, the outcome is always from Allah ﷻ. We can pray for Allah ﷻ to put *barakah* in our efforts, our planning and the way we are working. Ultimately whatever we gain is from Him.

Secondly, many people work as hard as you or I, but Allah ﷻ in His wisdom doesn't give them. يَبۡسُطُ ٱلرِّزۡقَ لِمَن يَشَآءُ. *He gives to whom He wills*. If and when we do gain success or wealth, what should we do? The lesson we take from these verses is to always connect the blessing with the source of the blessing, to the One who gave that blessing. Then we need to use it in the way that pleases Allah ﷻ, without being arrogant or showing off to people and avoiding feeling superior.

Thirdly, we need to use our wealth for the sake of Allah ﷻ, in the way that pleases Him. There is no harm in us using our wealth for our *dunya* with humility, and most importantly not using it to disobey Allah ﷻ. Our time in this world is very short and the story of Qarun has some profound lessons-where the punishment is the same or equal to the sin. Qarun was arrogant, Allah ﷻ made the Earth swallow him. This is the outcome of someone who was ungrateful, may Allah ﷻ protect us all.

We have to be very careful not to be like Qarun and check ourselves; could it be that we have one or two of his qualities? We need to ask Allah ﷻ to protect us when He gives us, as He has bestowed a lot of blessings on us. We need to make sure we always remember He is the source and make us among the grateful, as we know from the Qur'an where Allah ﷻ says: 'وَقَلِيلٞ مِّنۡ عِبَادِيَ ٱلشَّكُورُ. *Very few of my servants are grateful.*' (*Saba* 34:13)

May Allah ﷻ make us among those few who are grateful and make us patient. Amīn.

Points to reflect on:

- Keep a balanced view about our money and wealth: it is a resource from Allah ﷻ, He can give it to us or take it away
- Be mindful of how we use our money. The Qur'an calls for a middle way with using our wealth, neither wasteful nor tight-fisted

- Always keep the *akhirah* in mind in relation to our money. What can we do with it that is rewardable in the hereafter?
- Reflect on our own attitude and behaviour: do we stay the same whether we have money or wealth, or does it change our behaviour?
- Do we admire richer people over humble people with less material wealth? What are our values and perceptions about those who do and don't have wealth?

مَثَلُ الَّذِينَ يُنفِقُونَ أَمْوَالَهُمْ فِي سَبِيلِ اللَّهِ كَمَثَلِ حَبَّةٍ أَنبَتَتْ سَبْعَ سَنَابِلَ فِي
كُلِّ سُنبُلَةٍ مِّائَةُ حَبَّةٍ ۗ وَاللَّهُ يُضَاعِفُ لِمَن يَشَاءُ ۗ وَاللَّهُ وَاسِعٌ عَلِيمٌ ۝ الَّذِينَ
يُنفِقُونَ أَمْوَالَهُمْ فِي سَبِيلِ اللَّهِ ثُمَّ لَا يُتْبِعُونَ مَا أَنفَقُوا مَنًّا وَلَا أَذًى ۙ لَّهُمْ أَجْرُهُمْ
عِندَ رَبِّهِمْ وَلَا خَوْفٌ عَلَيْهِمْ وَلَا هُمْ يَحْزَنُونَ ۝ قَوْلٌ مَّعْرُوفٌ وَمَغْفِرَةٌ خَيْرٌ مِّن
صَدَقَةٍ يَتْبَعُهَا أَذًى ۗ وَاللَّهُ غَنِيٌّ حَلِيمٌ ۝

The parable of those who spend their wealth in Allah's way is that of a grain that produces seven clusters; in each cluster is a hundred grains. Allah multiplies for whom He wills. Allah is Bountiful and Knowledgeable. Those who spend their wealth in Allah's way, then do not follow up their charity with reminders of generosity or with insults—they will have their reward with their Lord—they have nothing to fear, nor will they grieve. Kind words and forgiveness are better than charity followed by insults. Allah is Rich and Clement.

(*al-Baqarah* 2:261-263)

Chapter 20

WHAT DOES THE QUR'AN SAY ABOUT FOOD AND WASTE?

One of the daily enjoyments of this life is eating and drinking. Is this addressed in the Qur'an? If it is, did Allah ﷻ set limits or boundaries around it? The answer, as you might expect, is yes. It is amazing that eating and drinking are mentioned as an order and encouragement from Allah ﷻ to consume, but within guidelines that He has set. We will take a closer look at what these are.

Food and gratitude:

يَا أَيُّهَا الَّذِينَ آمَنُوا كُلُوا مِنْ طَيِّبَاتِ مَا رَزَقْنَاكُمْ
وَاشْكُرُوا لِلَّهِ إِنْ كُنْتُمْ إِيَّاهُ تَعْبُدُونَ

O you who believe! Eat of the good things We have provided for you, and give thanks to Allah, if it is Him that you worship.

(*al-Baqarah* 2:172)

We are instructed here to eat from the pure, beautiful food Allah ﷻ has provided for us. At the same time we are told to be grateful to Allah ﷻ if we are truly among those who worship Him, and so the connection between eating and *ibadah* – worship is clearly made. This is followed, in the next verse with the limits on what we should not eat clearly explained:

إِنَّمَا حَرَّمَ عَلَيْكُمُ ٱلْمَيْتَةَ وَٱلدَّمَ وَلَحْمَ ٱلْخِنزِيرِ وَمَآ أُهِلَّ بِهِۦ لِغَيْرِ ٱللَّهِ ۖ فَمَنِ
ٱضْطُرَّ غَيْرَ بَاغٍ وَلَا عَادٍ فَلَآ إِثْمَ عَلَيْهِ ۚ إِنَّ ٱللَّهَ غَفُورٌ رَّحِيمٌ

He has only forbidden you carrion, blood, pig's meat, and animals over which any name other than God's has been invoked. But if anyone is forced to eat such things by hunger, rather than desire or excess, he commits no sin: God is most merciful and forgiving.

(*al-Baqarah* 2:173)

There are only a few things that the word *haram* is used for, and even here we are told in exceptional circumstances where ones life may be at threat this does not apply. Another point of note, is that the order to eat didn't just come down to believers, in the following verse the address is general to everyone: Allah ﷻ said,

يَا أَيُّهَا النَّاسُ كُلُوا مِمَّا فِي الْأَرْضِ حَلَالًا طَيِّبًا

O people! Eat of what is lawful and pure on the Earth.

(*al-Baqarah* 2:168)

Moderation in what we consume

The directions on what to eat and what to avoid is established for us. Hence when we eat and drink with the intention to follow these limits, we're actually obeying Allah ﷻ.

Allah ﷻ further sets certain boundaries through the following *ayaat*.

يَا بَنِي آدَمَ خُذُوا زِينَتَكُمْ عِندَ كُلِّ مَسْجِدٍ وَكُلُوا وَاشْرَبُوا
وَلَا تُسْرِفُوا ۚ إِنَّهُ لَا يُحِبُّ الْمُسْرِفِينَ

O Children of Adam! Dress appropriately at every place of worship. And eat and drink, but do not be excessive. He does not like those who squander.

(*al-A'raf* 7:31)

The children of Adam are addressed here to beautify themselves when we go to the masjid. Again, the same order exists, where we're told to eat and drink, and now the boundaries are put in: وَلَا تُسْرِفُوا - don't waste. After which Allah ﷻ places a guideline, إِنَّهُ لَا يُحِبُّ الْمُسْرِفِينَ- He does not like extravagance.

In chapter five we talked about the types of love in the Qur'an. Of these, the love of Allah ﷻ is what we want the most. As we know Allah ﷻ doesn't love those who waste, we really need to ask ourselves about our food waste. What does food waste mean for us? This applies to what we do, and how we eat, particularly when it is more than what we need. Do we eat to the point where it is harmful for us? Or do we do things in general that are wasteful and for show? Or could this be applied to ignoring the boundaries of what is permissible in what we consume and wear? These are a few things for us to ponder over from this verse.

Eating as an act of *ibadah*

When we are eating at home alone, or eating with the family, or we’re invited to a larger gathering and put food on our plate, we need to remember the following; that eating is an act of obeying Allah ﷻ. And if our intention is to obey Allah ﷻ, then this will become an act of worship and Allah ﷻ will reward us.

When we’re serving ourselves food we should consider whether the quantity we have placed on our plate is the right amount. If it’s too much what should come to mind is that over consuming displeases Allah ﷻ, and recalling these limits is an act of worship.

Prophetic advice about food

A very famous hadith of *Rasul Allah* ﷺ related by Imam al-Tirmidhi, is one in which he said:

ملأ ابنُ آدمَ وعاءً شرًا من بطنِه حسْبُ ابنِ آدمَ أُكلاتٌ يُقمْنَ صلبَه فإن كان لا محالةَ فثُلثٌ ‘ لطعامِه وثلثٌ لشرابِه وثلثٌ لنفسِه. Enough for the son of Adam, is a bite that will keep him going. So you don’t feel you’re too hungry, you can’t move or think. And If you have to eat, keep one-third for food, one-third for drink, and one-third for air.’

Another hadith of *Rasul Allah* ﷺ, to remind us anytime we are about to eat is:

إِنَّ أَكْثَرَ النَّاسِ شِبَعًا فِي الدُّنْيَا أَطْوَلُهُمْ جُوعًا يَوْمَ الْقِيَامَةِ

‘The people who eat to full satiation, they will be the people who are really hungry on the Day of Judgement.’ (al-Tirmidhi)

So when one stops at the point where they want to eat more, this hadith is a reminder not to eat to one’s full, in order to be from the people who will be fed on the Day of Judgement. We can look to the example of *Sayyidin* Umar ؓ and what he said about food and drink. He had the ability to live in luxury had he chosen to. He said, ‘by Allah, if I want, I would have dressed in the softest thing and I would have eaten the best food and would have lived the highest level of luxury. But I remembered a verse in the Qur’an where Allah ﷻ said:

On the Day when those who deny the truth are brought before the Fire, it will be said to them, 'You squandered the good things you were given in your Earthly life, you took your fill of pleasure there, so on this Day a punishment of shame is yours: you were arrogant on Earth without any right, and exceeded all limits.' (*al-Ahqaf* 46:20) [1]

A balanced way to consume

In life, we need to maintain balance. Allah ﷻ created us as an أُمَّةً وَسَطًا. We are 'a nation of the middle [path]', therefore we should avoid both extremes. When we come near to wastefulness, we should remember Allah ﷻ doesn't love those who waste. In addition, there is a verse in the Qur'an which gives another dimension to this:

إِنَّ الْمُبَذِّرِينَ كَانُوا إِخْوَانَ الشَّيَاطِينِ

The extravagant are brethren of the devils.

(*al-Isra* 17:27)

Those who waste, be that wasting time, food, energy, resources, are the brothers of *Shaytan*. Would anyone want to be a brother of *Shaytan* or a sister of *Shaytan*? The answer is unequivocally no.

As we covered in the previous chapter about money, keeping to the middle path with all our resources is the Qur'anic advice:

"And [they are] those who, when they spend, do so not excessively or sparingly but are ever between that, [justly] moderate"

(*al-Furqaan* 25:67)

To bring valuable change in our lives, we can make eating mindfully, a part of our *ibadah* - our acts of worship, besides the obligatory acts of worship such as prayer, fasting, reading the Qur'an, doing good deeds and giving in charity. We can make it a part of our *ibadah* that we're going to eat in a way that pleases Allah ﷻ with the intention that this is going to help us get closer to Allah ﷻ.

1 This *ayah* addresses the non-believer's however it shows the importance that *Sayyidina* Umar ؓ had for every single word in the Qur'an and how it may impact him.

May Allah ﷻ always make us from those who are grateful for all the blessings that Allah ﷻ has bestowed on us. Ya Rabbi Amīn.

Points to reflect on:

- Eating with the right intention, as an act of worship, can become a daily habit if we are mindful of this.
- Gratitude for what Allah ﷻ has provided will help us appreciate the blessing of food.
- Avoiding waste are signs of true faith and consciousness of Allah ﷻ and we will be rewarded for being conscious of this.
- Waste and ungratefulness are loved by *Shaytan* – this alone should motivate us to make a change.
- Can we make better food choices of eating what is *tayyib* 'pure' from the Earth? Choosing whole foods over processed foods is better for us, and is in keeping with the Qur'anic view.
- Are we staying within the clear limits set by Allah ﷻ of what is *halal* and *haram*? Doing so affects our health, spiritual and physical well-being.

فَلْيَنظُرِ الْإِنسَانُ إِلَىٰ طَعَامِهِ ۝ أَنَّا صَبَبْنَا الْمَاءَ صَبًّا ۝ ثُمَّ شَقَقْنَا الْأَرْضَ شَقًّا
۝ فَأَنبَتْنَا فِيهَا حَبًّا ۝ وَعِنَبًا وَقَضْبًا ۝ وَزَيْتُونًا وَنَخْلًا ۝ وَحَدَائِقَ غُلْبًا ۝
وَفَاكِهَةً وَأَبًّا ۝ مَّتَاعًا لَّكُمْ وَلِأَنْعَامِكُمْ ۝

وَصَاحِبَتِهِ وَبَنِيهِ ۝ وَأُمِّهِ وَأَبِيهِ ۝ يَوْمَ يَفِرُّ الْمَرْءُ مِنْ أَخِيهِ ۝
فَإِذَا جَاءَتِ الصَّاخَّةُ ۝ ضَاحِكَةٌ مُّسْتَبْشِرَةٌ ۝ وُجُوهٌ يَوْمَئِذٍ مُّسْفِرَةٌ ۝
لِكُلِّ امْرِئٍ مِّنْهُمْ يَوْمَئِذٍ شَأْنٌ يُغْنِيهِ أُولَٰئِكَ هُمُ الْكَفَرَةُ الْفَجَرَةُ ۝ تَرْهَقُهَا قَتَرَةٌ
۝ وَوُجُوهٌ يَوْمَئِذٍ عَلَيْهَا غَبَرَةٌ ۝

Let the human being look at his food. How We pour down water in abundance. Then crack the soil open. And grow in it grains. And grapes and herbs. And olives and dates. And luscious gardens. And fruits and vegetables. As sustenance for you and for your livestock. But when the Deafening Blast comes to pass. The Day when a person will flee from his brother. And his mother and his father. And his spouse and his children. Every one of them, on that Day, will have enough to preoccupy him. Some faces on that Day will be radiant. Laughing and rejoicing. And some faces on that Day will be covered with dust. Covered by darkness. These are the faithless, the wicked.

(*'Abasa* 80:24-42)

Chapter 21

DOES THE QUR'AN MENTION DIVORCE?

Going to weddings and hearing the good news of people getting married is a joyous part of life. Unfortunately, sometimes things don't go the way we expected or planned. Allah ﷻ knows this might happen and so He addresses the subject of divorce in the Qur'an. He frames it in a way that it is neither encouraged nor condemned, as sometimes it is inevitable. What do we need to learn from the Qur'an about divorce? What are the boundaries and where do the rights and responsibilities fall for the woman and the man?

Taqwa and rulings

There are two places in the Qur'an where the subject of divorce is covered in detail. One of them is in *Surah al-Baqarah*, and the other *Surah al-Talaq*, where Allah ﷻ covers divorce extensively. *Surah al-Talaq* emphasise, يَـٰٓأَيُّهَا ٱلنَّبِىُّ, where Allah ﷻ is addressing *Rasul Allah* ﷺ directly to emphasize the seriousness of this subject. The beginning of this chapters imparts a feeling of urgency to teach the Prophet Muhammad ﷺ about the rules and guidelines. There is a strong opinion that he actually divorced Hafsa, the daughter of *Sayyidina* Umar, and then he brought her back. The *surah* starts:

يَا أَيُّهَا النَّبِيُّ إِذَا طَلَّقْتُمُ النِّسَاءَ

O Prophet! If any of you divorce women.

(*al-Talaq* 65:1)

The *surah* proceeds with Allah ﷻ telling us what to be very careful about, such as the waiting period; the times a man cannot divorce the woman; what happens if she is pregnant; what happens if she is breastfeeding and the divorce happens. All these rulings include different scenarios, for example the way the waiting period is related to menstruation, or what happens in the case of a woman who may not menstruate.

One of the remarkable features of *Surah al-Talaq* which consists of twelve verses, is how Allah ﷻ mentions the word *taqwa* five times in different ways. Most commonly is, وَمَن يَتَّقِ ٱللَّهَ. – 'the person who practises *taqwa*,' because having *taqwa* – or God consciousness is not only internal, but evident in our actions too. Divorce is difficult. It's a testing situation, that often times involves harm and pain. The ego plays a role too and it is an emotional journey. In this context, the only way for us as human beings to conduct a divorce in the way that pleases Allah ﷻ is to remember *taqwa* of

Allah ﷻ; that He is watching. It is Allah ﷻ Who is allowing it, and gives us parameters. Those getting divorced are reminded they need to follow these boundaries. For example, one guideline in this *surah* is not to cause harm. In another part, we are directed: 'do not hold them', meaning don't divorce them so you cause more harm to them. He also taught us not to treat a woman in such a way that prevents her from marrying somebody else. Provision for the woman to remain in her home is also mentioned – this is all in the Qur'an.

One of the tests people face when getting divorced is the whispers of *Shaytan*; '*why should I do this, or why would I give that? I'm going to lose this; or why should I compromise…*' and so on. Allah ﷻ gives one of the most beautiful verses as an antidote to these whispers. *Rasul Allah* ﷺ noted that the following *ayah* is more than enough for the one who practises it. It is verse number two in *Surah al-Talaq*:

وَمَن يَتَّقِ ٱللَّهَ يَجۡعَل لَّهُۥ مَخۡرَجٗا

Whoever practises taqwa,
Allah will make a way out for him.

(*al-Talaq* 65: 2)

There are so many meanings of this word 'way out'. It could be someone has financial issues during a divorce and being conscious of Allah ﷻ and obeying Him, will facilitate or remove this problem. By not obeying Allah ﷻ in the divorce, a person instead could incur financial loss when they go against His ruling. Remember, obeying Allah ﷻ and being Allah ﷻ conscious leads to Him paving a way out, because going through a divorce makes life very difficult. Allah ﷻ says:

وَمَن يَتَّقِ ٱللَّهَ يَجۡعَل لَّهُۥ مِنۡ أَمۡرِهِۦ يُسۡرٗا

If you're going to follow Allah's rule, Allah will make it easy for you.

(*Al-Talaq* 65:4)

Another interesting feature of *Surah al-Talaq*, is that the name of Allah ﷻ, is repeated many times in it. Within the verses, Allah ﷻ teaches us more lessons by showing the result of what happened to a nation that disobeyed Him.

عَتَتْ عَنْ أَمْرِ رَبِّهَا،
فَذَاقَتْ وَبَالَ أَمْرِهَا

They absolutely did not obey Allah. They paid the price for it.

(*al-Talaq* 65: 8-9)

At the end of *Surah al-Talaq*, our attention is turned towards Who Allah ﷻ is:

ٱللَّهُ ٱلَّذِى خَلَقَ سَبْعَ سَمَٰوَٰتٍ وَمِنَ ٱلْأَرْضِ مِثْلَهُنَّ يَتَنَزَّلُ ٱلْأَمْرُ بَيْنَهُنَّ لِتَعْلَمُوٓا۟ أَنَّ
ٱللَّهَ عَلَىٰ كُلِّ شَىْءٍ قَدِيرٌ وَأَنَّ ٱللَّهَ قَدْ أَحَاطَ بِكُلِّ شَىْءٍ عِلْمًۢا ١٢

It is God who created seven heavens and a similar [number] of Earths. His command descends throughout them. So you should realise that He has power over all things and that His knowledge encompasses everything.

(*al-Talaq* 65:12)

For the person going through a divorce, they can be reassured that Allah ﷻ knows the suffering he or she is going through. He knows the painful process people are going through and the feeling of failure people sometimes feel, as أَنَّ ٱللَّهَ عَلَىٰ كُلِّ شَىْءٍ قَدِيرٌ *He has knowledge of it all.*

Islam is a beautiful religion that touches on the realities we face. Islam has a sublime nature which teaches us how to deal with what comes our way. What we all need to learn is when we go through this difficult time, we need to remember Allah ﷻ and learn what Allah ﷻ has taught each and every one of the believers in the Qur'an. If we obey Him ﷻ and follow it, even if externally it's going to make us feel that we may be losing something, we are reminded: وَمَن يَتَّقِ اللَّهِ يَجْعَلْ لَهُ مَخْرَجًا. '*Whoever practises Allah consciousness, Allah will find a way for them.*'

May Allah ﷻ protect all the marriages. May Allah ﷻ make divorce a way that will bring *khair* (good). Everything that comes from Allah ﷻ is *khair*. Everything Allah ﷻ allows is *khair*, even if externally it doesn't first appear like this. Ya Rabbi Amīn.

Points to reflect on:

- The Qur'an addresses our testing times, so we should turn to the Qur'an first to seek comfort and guidance.
- Rights and responsibilities in marriage and divorce are sacred. Remembering this, and acting accordingly, will ease difficulties when they arise.
- *Taqwa* – God consciousness at all times, is the key ingredient to do justice to both sides when they part ways.
- Islam protects women and children in Divine law when there is a divorce. Are we upholding these principles when a separation takes place?
- A well-known principle applies to divorce and life generally: Allah ﷻ promises ease and help to those who obey His limits.

وَإِذَا طَلَّقْتُمُ النِّسَاءَ فَبَلَغْنَ أَجَلَهُنَّ فَأَمْسِكُوهُنَّ بِمَعْرُوفٍ أَوْ سَرِّحُوهُنَّ
بِمَعْرُوفٍ ۚ وَلَا تُمْسِكُوهُنَّ ضِرَارًا لِتَعْتَدُوا ۚ وَمَنْ يَفْعَلْ ذَٰلِكَ فَقَدْ ظَلَمَ نَفْسَهُ ۚ وَلَا
تَتَّخِذُوا آيَاتِ اللَّهِ هُزُوًا ۚ وَاذْكُرُوا نِعْمَتَ اللَّهِ عَلَيْكُمْ وَمَا أَنْزَلَ عَلَيْكُمْ مِنَ الْكِتَابِ
وَالْحِكْمَةِ يَعِظُكُمْ بِهِ ۚ وَاتَّقُوا اللَّهَ وَاعْلَمُوا أَنَّ اللَّهَ بِكُلِّ شَيْءٍ عَلِيمٌ ۝ وَإِذَا
طَلَّقْتُمُ النِّسَاءَ فَبَلَغْنَ أَجَلَهُنَّ فَلَا تَعْضُلُوهُنَّ أَنْ يَنْكِحْنَ أَزْوَاجَهُنَّ إِذَا تَرَاضَوْا
بَيْنَهُمْ بِالْمَعْرُوفِ ۗ ذَٰلِكَ يُوعَظُ بِهِ مَنْ كَانَ مِنْكُمْ يُؤْمِنُ بِاللَّهِ وَالْيَوْمِ الْآخِرِ ۗ ذَٰلِكُمْ
أَزْكَىٰ لَكُمْ وَأَطْهَرُ ۗ وَاللَّهُ يَعْلَمُ وَأَنْتُمْ لَا تَعْلَمُونَ ۝

And when you have divorced women, and they have reached their term, either retain them amicably or release them amicably. But do not retain them to hurt them and commit aggression. Whoever does that has wronged himself. And do not take Allah's revelations for a joke. And remember Allah's blessing upon you, and that He revealed to you the Scripture and Wisdom, to teach you. And be cautious of Allah, and know that Allah knows everything. When you have divorced women, and they have reached their term, do not prevent them from marrying their husbands, provided they mutually agree on fair terms. This is enjoined on whomever among you believes in Allah and the Last Day. That is purer for you, and more decent. Allah knows, and you do not know.

(*al-Baqarah* 2:231-232)

Chapter 22

DOES THE QUR'AN MENTION JEALOUSY AND ENVY?

In our daily lives on this Earth we all face challenges. In previous chapters we explored the trials associated with money; the pressures during marriage; and the struggles that can result in divorce. Some of the greatest difficulties we face though, are internal, to do with our emotions. Are difficult emotions mentioned in the Qur'an? Yes, Allah ﷻ does mention a range of difficult feelings such as envy and jealousy, and highlights the connection between experiencing an emotion and how we react to it.

Envy & Jealousy between siblings

In *Surah al-Ma'idah*, The Table, Allah ﷻ shows us through the dialogue between two brothers – Habil and Qabil, how a negative feeling from one brother towards the other resulted in him saying and doing things that led to the first crime on this Earth. The verse starts with Allah ﷻ telling the *Rasul Allah* ﷺ to inform all people about this.

وَٱتْلُ عَلَيْهِمْ نَبَأَ ٱبْنَيْ ءَادَمَ بِٱلْحَقِّ.

(Prophet) tell them the truth about the story of the two sons of Adam.

إِذْ قَرَّبَا قُرْبَانًا.

When both offered to Allah ﷻ, a sacrifice

فَتُقُبِّلَ مِنْ أَحَدِهِمَا.

It was accepted from one of them.

وَلَمْ يُتَقَبَّلْ مِنَ ٱلْأَخَرِ

and was not accepted from the other.

(*al-Ma'idah* 5:27)

The *qurbani* – sacrifice that was offered was exactly the same and done as an act to get closer to Allah ﷻ. What happened when Qabil's sacrifice wasn't accepted? The rest of the verse tells us:

قَالَ لَأَقْتُلَنَّكَ.

One angrily said 'I will kill you.'

This immediate response from Qabil whose sacrifice was rejected showed his anger and jealousy which led to the threat to kill. In response, his brother Habil replied:

' قَالَ إِنَّمَا يَتَقَبَّلُ ٱللَّهُ مِنَ ٱلْمُتَّقِينَ.

Allah only accepts the sacrifices of those who have taqwa, Allah conscious.

لَئِنۢ بَسَطتَ إِلَيَّ يَدَكَ لِتَقْتُلَنِى مَآ أَنَا۠ بِبَاسِطٍ يَدِىَ إِلَيْكَ
لِأَقْتُلَكَ ۖ إِنِّىٓ أَخَافُ ٱللَّهَ رَبَّ ٱلْعَـٰلَمِينَ

If you raise your hand to kill me, I will not raise mine to kill you.
I fear Allah, Lord of all worlds.

(*al-Ma'idah* 5:27-28)

Emotions in our daily lives

There are several things to reflect on here; we don't know where this happened, nor are the names in the Qur'an[1] because these details of the incident are not relevant. What we are supposed to pay attention to is the Qur'an's message. Allah ﷻ wants us to learn about the feelings of envy and jealousy. Qabil was jealous because Allah ﷻ didn't accept the sacrifice from him but did accept it from his brother. In our daily lives we encounter these situations regularly and people experience these emotions when they compare. For example *why does someone have something I don't have? Why has he or she been given so much money, and I haven't? Or, why was a particular colleague promoted and I was not? Why have they been given children, and I am not given the same?* It could be anything that one person has, which is perceived as good, which another didn't receive – the emotion of envy or jealousy then surfaces.

---

1 The names Habil and Qabil are not in the Qur'an are found in the Tafsir of Ibn Kathir.

A cure to envy: *Taqwa*

The reaction to this should be Allah ﷻ is عادل, Allah is Just. When Allah ﷻ gives to someone and doesn't give to the other it is out of His justice. He alone knows what's good for us or not. However, Qabil didn't understand it this way. His immediate feelings of rage and anger – which is the main issue here, was translated to the act of a major sin: لَأَقْتُلَنَّكَ, *'I am going to kill you'*. This response also carries the message here, that when one feels anger or jealousy, it is best not to act on it, because sometimes acting out of these emotions can lead to a major sin. This killing was the first crime on this Earth.

Allah ﷻ teaches us through the God conscious brother, how to respond to an act of aggression in a way that is pleasing to Him: Habil explained to his brother why Allah ﷻ accepted his sacrifice but not his brothers: *taqwa* and his relationship with Allah ﷻ. Ibn Kathir commented in his *tafsir* that the sacrifice of Qabil was from his vegetation, whereas Habil sacrificed his best ram. The message we get is if we are Allah conscious with fear and hope in Him, our actions will be accepted.

We now learn why Allah ﷻ accepted the pious brother's sacrifice, but not his siblings. Being the righteous man he was, went beyond his relationship with Allah ﷻ, and extended to his relationship with others too. How do we respond to acts of aggression against us? Are we unjust and reactive or do we respond with leaving the matter to Allah ﷻ.

إِنِّيٓ أُرِيدُ أَن تَبُوٓأَ بِإِثۡمِي وَإِثۡمِكَ فَتَكُونَ مِنۡ أَصۡحَٰبِ ٱلنَّارِۚ وَذَٰلِكَ جَزَٰٓؤُاْ ٱلظَّٰلِمِينَ

'and I would rather you were burdened with my sins as well as yours and became an inhabitant of the Fire: such is the evildoers' reward.'

(*al-Ma'idah* 5:29)

After stating this, he reminds his brother of the fate of someone choosing to be a wrongdoer and the ultimate destination of *Jahanam*.

The *nafs* and emotions

فَطَوَّعَتۡ لَهُۥ نَفۡسُهُۥ قَتۡلَ أَخِيهِ فَقَتَلَهُۥ فَأَصۡبَحَ مِنَ ٱلۡخَٰسِرِينَ ۝

But his soul prompted him to kill his brother: so he killed him and became one of the losers.

(*al-Ma'idah* 5:30)

This is a sublime way to talk about our feelings and our *nafs*, to explain why people do the things they do. فَطَوَّعَتْ '*tawwa'at*' implies Qabil didn't find killing his brother easy to do and he wasn't pleased to do this crime. His lower *nafs*, that calls to evil, encouraged him to do something he was hesitant to do. In this way فَطَوَّعَتْ reminds us that something wrong may seem bad or difficult at first, but one's *nafs* can change that into making it easier to do.

فَبَعَثَ ٱللَّهُ غُرَابًا يَبْحَثُ فِى ٱلْأَرْضِ لِيُرِيَهُۥ كَيْفَ يُوَٰرِى سَوْءَةَ أَخِيهِ ۚ قَالَ يَٰوَيْلَتَىٰٓ أَعَجَزْتُ أَنْ أَكُونَ مِثْلَ هَٰذَا ٱلْغُرَابِ فَأُوَٰرِىَ سَوْءَةَ أَخِى ۖ فَأَصْبَحَ مِنَ ٱلنَّٰدِمِينَ ۝

God sent a raven to scratch up the ground and show him how to cover his brother's corpse and he said, 'Woe is me! Could I not have been like this raven and covered up my brother's body?' He became remorseful.

(*al-Ma'idah* 5:31)

Once he killed Habil, he didn't know what to do with his body, so Allah ﷻ, sent a raven to show him what to do with it. What do we learn from this? Our feelings are recognised in the Qur'an, even if they are negative. We are cautioned to be careful and react to a situation with control. When we connect everything with Allah ﷻ, whether He gives or withholds, we know He is the Most Just – *Al-Adl*, and there will be *khayr* – good in it for us, whether this is obvious or not. And when we have these feelings recurring, our task is not to *act* on these emotions. How can we do that? We can change our state by following the guidance our *Rasul Allah* ﷺ gave us. He ﷺ said if we are in a state of anger, we should make *wudu*. If we are standing, then we should sit down, if sitting and angry, we should lie down – the main point is to change our state. The underlying reminder to ourselves, is not to react when we experience negative feelings because it may lead to major sins.

May Allah ﷻ protect us and teach us and may Allah ﷻ make it easy for us. Amīn.

Points to reflect on:

- Allah ﷻ is Just *Al – Adl*, when we recall this in our life we will find contentment in what He gives and what He withholds.
- When we see something someone else has which we desire, make *du'a* for them and ask Allah ﷻ to be blessed with it too, if it is good for you.
- The emotions we feel are normal, what matters is how we react to negative feelings, and we need to avoid taking actions based on these feelings.
- Allah ﷻ is *Ar-Razaaq* – The Provider, when we recall this, we find peace in the differences between what we and others have. Not all provision is visible, and Allah ﷻ provides in different ways to us all.
- Responding to anger calmly is the God conscious way to reply to someone's aggression.
- Allah ﷻ accepts the efforts of those who are conscious of Him.
- Some of the most difficult feelings occur between family members – this is common. God consciousness will help to keep the *nafs* in check and not overcome by whispers from the lower self.

قڤُلْ أَعُوذُ بِرَبِّ الْفَلَقِ ۞ مِنْ شَرِّ مَا خَلَقَ ۞ وَمِنْ شَرِّ غَاسِقٍ إِذَا وَقَبَ ۞ وَمِنْ
شَرِّ النَّفَّاثَاتِ فِي الْعُقَدِ ۞ وَمِنْ شَرِّ حَاسِدٍ إِذَا حَسَدَ

Say, "I seek refuge in the Lord of Daybreak. From the evil of what He created. And from the evil of the darkness as it gathers. And from the evil of those who practise sorcery. And from the evil of an envier when he envies."

(*al-Falaq* 113:1-5)

Chapter 23

IS SUCCESS MENTIONED IN THE QUR'AN?

Every one of us wants to be successful in some way or another. Whether this is in using our skills, in raising our family, in working for a cause- there's nothing wrong with wanting to achieve this with *ihsan* -excellence. Is success a concept we find in the Qur'an? Yes, several verses define and frame success. In *Surah al-Muminoon* Allah ﷻ begins by describing success. How does He explain success for believers?

The qualities of the successful believers

قَدْ أَفْلَحَ الْمُؤْمِنُونَ. *Indeed, the believers are successful* (*al-Muminoon* 23:1). And then He gives us the criteria: الَّذِينَ هُمْ فِى صَلَاتِهِمْ خَـٰشِعُونَ, *those who are humbled in their prayers* (*al-Muminoon* 23:2).

Salah is the first measure of success in the sight of Allah ﷻ so He prioritised this in the Qur'an. 'خَـٰشِعُونَ,' '*Khushu*'means they are humble, have submitted to Allah ﷻ and are focused during their *Salah*.

Next we are told what the success factors in life are, outside of *ibadah*-worship.

وَٱلَّذِينَ هُمْ عَنِ ٱللَّغْوِ مُعْرِضُونَ *Who stay away from vain talk.* (*al-Muminoon* 23:3) which includes talk that is of no benefit, and even more so, conversation that is *haram*-unlawful talk.

وَٱلَّذِينَ هُمْ لِلزَّكَوٰةِ فَـٰعِلُونَ *Who give Zakat* (*al-Muminoon* 23:4). Now we are brought back to the concept of money and making sure we purify it, as an act of worship through giving Zakat. The meaning here emphasise that they do this *without* any hesitation.

وَٱلَّذِينَ هُمْ لِفُرُوجِهِمْ حَـٰفِظُونَ *Who guard their chastity* (*al-Muminoon* 23:5). The successful believers prioritise their modesty, dress and interactions in the way that pleases Allah ﷻ, with the exception of what is permissible between spouses and *mahram* (those we can't marry), as we covered in chapter fifteen on the dress code. This is followed by another significant concept that will give us success in the *dunya* and *akhirah*:

وَٱلَّذِينَ هُمْ لِأَمَـٰنَـٰتِهِمْ وَعَهْدِهِمْ رَٰعُونَ *Who are faithful to their trusts and contracts.* (*al-Muminoon* 23:8).

Allah ﷻ names honouring our promises and covenants and keeping our word as another important criteria. We can ask ourselves about our own daily interactions: *do I keep appointments? If I say I'm coming at eight, do I arrive on time? Do I communicate to say if I am going to be late? Do I reply to someone's message I promised to return? Am I trusted to keep a secret confidential?* These everyday situations, if conducted according to the guidelines laid down by Allah ﷻ, are a sign of success in this *dunya* and *akhirah*. Therefore Allah ﷻ highlighted, keeping someone's trust, as an act of worship in the Qur'an.

وَٱلَّذِينَ هُمْ عَلَىٰ صَلَوَٰتِهِمْ يُحَافِظُونَ

And regularly perform prayers. (al-Muminoon 23:9).

أُوْلَٰٓئِكَ هُمُ ٱلْوَٰرِثُونَ ١٠
ٱلَّذِينَ يَرِثُونَ ٱلْفِرْدَوْسَ هُمْ فِيهَا خَٰلِدُونَ ١١

Such people are true heirs, they will inherit Paradise, living in it forever.

(*al-Muminoon* 23:10-11)

The *Surah* started with *salah* and ends with *salah*. Successful believers are those who really guard their *salah*, as it's a priority over and above anything else in this world.

Success and *Jannah*

Allah ﷻ says in *Surah al-Imran*

فَمَن زُحْزِحَ عَنِ ٱلنَّارِ وَأُدْخِلَ ٱلْجَنَّةَ فَقَدْ فَازَ
وَمَا ٱلْحَيَوٰةُ ٱلدُّنْيَآ إِلَّا مَتَٰعُ ٱلْغُرُورِ

Whoever is swayed from the Fire, and admitted to Paradise, has won. This worldly life is no more than a deception.

(*al-Imran* 3:185)

The words Allah ﷻ uses are, فَمَن زُحْزِح, which implies someone being pulled away from danger زُحْزِحَ عَنِ النَّارِ which in this verse is the hellfire.

وَأُدْخِلَ الْجَنَّةِ, and they enter *Jannah*. So success is when everything we do in this life is going to move us away from the hellfire and towards *Jannah*.

Therefore, when we make something a priority in our life in order to be successful, the first question that should come to our mind is: *what will this do for me in the akhirah?* Even if what we plan is successful by worldly standards such as wealth and careers it needs to be accompanied by considering the *akhirah* – the hereafter. Whatever we prioritise should not move us closer to the hellfire, but instead help to keep us away from it. May Allah ﷻ protect us all.

Obeying Allah ﷻ and His Messenger ﷺ

One practical advice that Allah ﷻ told us in the Qur'an which helps us to achieve success in the *dunya* and *akhirah* is:

وَمَن يُطِعِ ٱللَّهَ وَرَسُولَهُۥ فَقَدْ فَازَ فَوْزًا عَظِيمًا

Whoever obeys Allah and His Messenger has achieved great success.

(*al-Ahzab* 33:71)

Allah ﷻ addresses everybody here, men and women, يُطِعِ, to obey. This verse is a very general statement emphasising with فَقَدْ which means 'indeed', obeying Allah ﷻ and the Messenger ﷺ, will lead to فَوْزًا, success. This type of a success is also described as a 'great success, فَازَ فَوْزًا عَظِيمًا.' What do we need to do to be successful? We need to focus and have goals, in fact the Prophet ﷺ encouraged us when he said:

المؤمنُ القويُّ خيرٌ وأحبُّ إلى الله من المؤمنِ الضَّعيفِ.

'The strong believer is better than the weak believer, and there is goodness in both.'

Strength could be in many things; strength in being educated, and in having status, and money or wealth. As long as what Allah ﷻ gives us in the *dunya* leads us to *Jannah*, then we can categorise this as true success. If what is called 'success' in this world takes us away from Allah ﷻ, and if it becomes the reason we don't achieve *Jannah*, or are delayed in going to *Jannah*, then we could be one of those who regret:

‘ رَبِّ ارْجِعُونِ۔ لَعَلِّىٓ أَعْمَلُ صَـٰلِحاً فِيمَا تَرَكْتُ كَلَّا

My Lord, send me back, so that I may work righteousness in what I neglected.'

(*al-Muminoon* 23:99-100).

This verse shows us the situation of a person in the *akhirah* wishing they could go back to this world and change, and do much better in earning good deeds.

As Muslims we should be encouraged to know success is an Islamic concept. Believers were absolutely successful in their lives; the *Sahabah* were successful, *Rasul Allah* ﷺ was especially successful. For our benefit, the question we need to bear in mind is what *kind* of success do we seek and what fruits of success will this bring us in the *akhirah*?

May Allah ﷻ help us, Ya Rabbi to learn and then practise what we learn. May Allah ﷻ make us all successful both in *dunya* and *akhirah*, Ya Rabbi. Amīn.

Points to reflect on:

- How do we discuss our goals for the future? What does success look like in our lives?
- Aligning our idea of success with the Qur'an's definition of success helps us in our daily lives in the *dunya* and for the *akhirah*.
- Focusing on our *salah* is the first priority to be successful, what can we improve about our *salah*, perhaps our timing or *khushu*?
- When we're in a social setting, we can stay vigilant with what we say and hear to avoid being someone who indulges in vain talk. This will help us achieve the ultimate success in the *akhirah*.
- How careful are we with the trusts and promises we make? We can check this on a daily basis and do our best to abide by these.
- Obedience to Allah ﷻ and His Messenger ﷺ is how we will gain ever-lasting success in the hereafter.

ذَٰلِكَ ٱلْكِتَـٰبُ لَا رَيْبَ ۛ فِيهِ ۛ هُدًى لِّلْمُتَّقِينَ ۝
ٱلَّذِينَ يُؤْمِنُونَ بِٱلْغَيْبِ وَيُقِيمُونَ ٱلصَّلَوٰةَ وَمِمَّا رَزَقْنَـٰهُمْ يُنفِقُونَ ۝
وَٱلَّذِينَ يُؤْمِنُونَ بِمَآ أُنزِلَ إِلَيْكَ وَمَآ أُنزِلَ مِن قَبْلِكَ وَبِٱلْـَٔاخِرَةِ هُمْ يُوقِنُونَ ۝
أُو۟لَـٰٓئِكَ عَلَىٰ هُدًى مِّن رَّبِّهِمْ ۖ وَأُو۟لَـٰٓئِكَ هُمُ ٱلْمُفْلِحُونَ ۝

"This is the Book about which there is no doubt, a guidance for those conscious of Allah – Who believe in the unseen, establish prayer, and spend out of what We have provided for them, And who believe in what has been revealed to you, [O Muhammad], and what was revealed before you, and of the Hereafter they are certain [in faith]. Those are upon [right] guidance from their Lord, and it is those who are the successful."

(*al-Baqarah* 2:2-5)

Chapter 24

WHAT DOES THE QUR'AN SAY ABOUT FAILURE?

One of the common questions a person asks in this world is about their success or failure; have I succeeded, or have I failed? Like all the questions in the previous chapters, this subject is also answered in the Qur'an. Allah ﷻ teaches us how to think about tests and trials, as in this verse in *Surah al-Hajj*:

وَمِنَ ٱلنَّاسِ مَن يَعْبُدُ ٱللَّهَ عَلَىٰ حَرْفٍ فَإِنْ أَصَابَهُۥ خَيْرٌ ٱطْمَأَنَّ بِهِۦ وَإِنْ أَصَابَتْهُ فِتْنَةٌ ٱنقَلَبَ عَلَىٰ وَجْهِهِۦ خَسِرَ ٱلدُّنْيَا وَٱلْءَاخِرَةَ ذَٰلِكَ هُوَ ٱلْخُسْرَانُ ٱلْمُبِينُ

"And of the people is he who worships Allāh on an edge. If he is touched by good, he is reassured by it; but if he is struck by trial, he turns his face [to unbelief]. He has lost [this] world and the Hereafter. That is what is the manifest loss."

(*al-Hajj* 22:11)

A person on the edge

This verse describes a person who worships Allah ﷻ 'on the edge, at the border. فَإِنْ أَصَابَهُۥ خَيْرٌ.' If goodness happens to him, ٱطْمَأَنَّ بِهِۦ he is very content with Islam. وَإِنْ أَصَابَتْهُ فِتْنَةٌ, But when faced with trials and failure, or issues he dislikes, he turns his back on the *deen*. 'On the edge' is also explained by Qatadah, Mujahid and others as 'in doubt'. Another interpretation suggests this is a person who enters the faith at the very edge, like the edge of a mountain, only staying if they find what they like, otherwise they are quick to leave.

Allah ﷻ is saying in this *ayah*: خَسِرَ ٱلدُّنْيَا وَٱلْءَاخِرَةَ, *this person has lost this life and the hereafter*. ذَٰلِكَ هُوَ ٱلْخُسْرَانُ ٱلْمُبِينُ, *that is indeed the clear loss, a real failure*.

Tests and trials

As human beings, we go through trials, especially when we find Islam and become attached to it. As Muslims, our living is in accordance to Allah's ﷻ Will which means making changes in our lives and being 'different' from others around us. When we experience tests, it can feel like the people who practise the *deen* are tested more than the people who do not. It can sometimes feel like the people who disbelieve are not tested, and have everything in *dunya*.

Allah ﷻ is telling us that tests are going to come, and these will be the litmus paper for us to show Allah ﷻ our sincerity to this religion. Tests or '*fitna*', as Allah ﷻ used in this verse, could be affliction, disease, loss of a loved one, or loss of a business, and all these are not seen as failures in the sight of Allah ﷻ. We may however, look at them as failures in this life, by our human measures. But in the sight of Allah ﷻ, this is not necessarily the case. Allah ﷻ is teaching us in the Qur'an through this verse that everything depends on how we respond to these trials. Will it result in us turning our back on our faith? Are we going to move away from Allah ﷻ? Or will we draw closer to Allah ﷻ because of this test and what happened?

This verse in *Surah al-Hajj* paints a picture of a person who weighs up faith as profit or loss. If it's someone who has achieved, for example they have a good business, have money and children, then they see this as success in life and the *akhirah*. And if the opposite occurs; there's loss in one's business or wealth or family, then this is seen as a failure. So when they experience good, then all is fine. If tests happen, that's equated to failure and causes them to change their relationship with Allah ﷻ. This is failure, in *dunya* and *akhirah* because this person has moved away from Allah ﷻ when they are tested.

Muffasir have further explained that the person who turns away from Allah ﷻ when tested, is deprived of trust, reassurance and contentment, in addition to his loss of wealth, children, health or other losses. Allah ﷻ requires His servants to demonstrate their trust in Him, to patiently persevere in the face of adversity, as well as to dedicate their lives to His cause and to His will.

This leads to the question of why Allah ﷻ tests us. There are many reasons for this, one of which is given in these verses of *Surah al-Ankabut* where Allah ﷻ says;

أَحَسِبَ النَّاسُ أَنْ يُتْرَكُوا أَنْ يَقُولُوا آمَنَّا وَهُمْ لَا يُفْتَنُونَ ۝ وَلَقَدْ فَتَنَّا الَّذِينَ مِنْ قَبْلِهِمْ ۖ فَلَيَعْلَمَنَّ اللَّهُ الَّذِينَ صَدَقُوا وَلَيَعْلَمَنَّ الْكَاذِبِينَ

Do people think they will be left alone to say, "We believe," without being tested? We tested those before them. Allah certainly knows those who are thankful, and He certainly knows the liars.
(*al-Ankabut* 29:2-3)

Allah's ﷻ test will show a person's real faith versus their 'on the edge' faith, or worse, their hypocrisy. Therefore in order to not fail, this is what we need to do. When we experience a test, we're going to tell ourselves, this is from Allah ﷻ and everything that comes from Allah ﷻ is *khayr*'. He is the Most Merciful. He is the Most Beloved. He is the One who loves His servants and the One who doesn't want to punish His servants. Sometimes we can see the message and the reason. Yet other times we can't, and need to trust in Allah's ﷻ plan.

Responding to the test

Our response should always be accepting the test and challenge, since it is from Allah ﷻ. We can reflect on what Allah ﷻ wants from us and be as content as one can be. We can be grateful for the test or failure that brings us back to Allah ﷻ. We can remind ourselves that our *du'a* should be improved, our connection to Him ﷻ should be stronger and our *salah* should be better. If we can respond in this way, then that's a success in this *dunya* because we took the test with the right attitude, when the reality is there's no choice to change it. The most important thing to remember is when we meet Allah ﷻ, all these tests will be in our book as a sign of accomplishment because it will be multiplied as good deeds. If we don't do that, and instead complain, weaken our faith or reject it, it won't change the test. We will still have to go through it, but unfortunately, we will lose in the *akhirah*.

May Allah ﷻ give us the insight to see that every test in this life is from Allah ﷻ and should bring us closer to Him. And may Allah ﷻ make it easy for everyone who's going through a test. Amīn.

Practical lessons

- The biggest failure in this world is the failure of abandoning the *deen*. It is not losing money, stocks or other assets.

- The opposite is also true. The biggest success in this world is the success in pleasing Allah ﷻ and preserving our *deen*.

- We need to find answers in our *deen* which will help us submit our heart and resolve doubts.

Questions to help us when tested:

◊ Do I worship Allah ﷻ the same whether I am happy and sad?

◊ Is my *Iman* the same no matter what I am going through in my life?

◊ Do I love Allah ﷻ the same when He gives me what I want and when He ﷻ doesn't give me what I want?

◊ How much proof do I need to submit fully and completely to Allah ﷻ, and when is the time to have my heart strongly attached to Allah ﷻ?

We need to clarify the difference between how everyone perceives 'failure' and what the Qur'an calls failure. How does this change the way we see ourselves and our past?

فَٱذْكُرُونِىٓ أَذْكُرْكُمْ وَٱشْكُرُوا۟ لِى وَلَا تَكْفُرُونِ ۝

يَـٰٓأَيُّهَا ٱلَّذِينَ ءَامَنُوا۟ ٱسْتَعِينُوا۟ بِٱلصَّبْرِ وَٱلصَّلَوٰةِ ۚ إِنَّ ٱللَّهَ مَعَ ٱلصَّـٰبِرِينَ ۝

So remember Me; I will remember you.
Be thankful to Me, and never ungrateful.
You who believe, seek help through steadfastness and prayer,
for God is with the steadfast.

(*Surah al-Baqarah* 2:152-153)

Chapter 25

ARE OUR FEELINGS EXPLORED IN THE QUR'AN?

One of the most common problems human beings are suffering from in contemporary times are feelings of sadness, anxiety, depression and restlessness. Does the Qur'an address these emotions? Yes, the Qur'an addresses all these feelings and has remedies for them too.

Confirming our feelings

Allah ﷻ affirmed this in *Surah al-Ma'arij* – The Stairways to Heaven:

إِنَّ ٱلْإِنسَـٰنَ خُلِقَ هَلُوعًا

Man was truly created anxious:

إِذَا مَسَّهُ ٱلشَّرُّ جَزُوعًا

he is fretful when misfortune touches him,

وَإِذَا مَسَّهُ ٱلْخَيْرُ مَنُوعًا

but tight-fisted when good fortune comes his way.

إِلَّا ٱلْمُصَلِّينَ

Except those who pray

(*al-Ma'arij* 70:19 -22)

We are being told about our state: that the human being was created with an inner characteristic of, هَلُوْعًا restlessness, and we can despair when things are uncomfortable and test us, but when Allah ﷻ gives us ease and we live a comfortable life, we can become miserly and forget Him. And then we are reminded that there are people who are an exception to this: it's those who are consistent in their *salah*. The verses which follow continue to list the qualities of those who are exceptional; people who help the deprived, keep trusts and give honest testimony amongst other virtues. (*al-Ma'arij* 70: 23 -33)

Prophets felt fear

The fact that we have this feeling of restlessness inside us, including anxiety, is usually about the unknown, of the future. People worry about an exam tomorrow, an impending interview next week, a delivery scheduled in a few days time – it's usually about something we are waiting for. Amazingly, Allah ﷻ mentioned the feeling of fear in the Qur'an as a natural emotion. This is mentioned in many Prophets' stories. We read of fear repeatedly, for example when we come to the story of *Sayyidina* Musa ﵇. Allah ﷻ, relates the scene to us when *Sayyidina* Musa ﵇ was told to go and invite the people of Pharaoh to worship Allah ﷻ, and he replied:

قَالَ رَبِّ إِنِّىٓ أَخَافُ أَن يُكَذِّبُونِ ۝

Moses said, 'My Lord, I fear they will call me a liar

وَيَضِيقُ صَدْرِى وَلَا يَنطَلِقُ لِسَانِى فَأَرْسِلْ إِلَىٰ هَٰرُونَ ۝

and I will feel stressed and tongue-tied, so send Aaron too;

وَلَهُمْ عَلَيَّ ذَنبٌ فَأَخَافُ أَن يَقْتُلُونِ ۝

Furthermore they have a charge against me, so I fear they may kill me.

(*ash-Shu'raa* 26:12-14).

Musa ﵇ expressed to Allah ﷻ that he was scared and worried firstly because he won't be believed. Secondly, because he had committed a crime of accidentally killing one of their people and he was afraid they would retaliate and take his life.

Sayyidina Ibrahim ﵇, *Khalilur Rahman*, the most beloved human being to Allah ﷻ, and the closest, and *Abul Anbiya*-the father of the prophets, the one who brought *Tawheed*-the oneness of Allah, also had this natural feeling.

When he saw the angels coming in the form of human beings, and he offered them food, he became afraid when he saw they didn't partake in the food he offered.

فَلَمَّا رَءَآ أَيْدِيَهُمْ لَا تَصِلُ إِلَيْهِ نَكِرَهُمْ وَأَوْجَسَ مِنْهُمْ خِيفَةً ۚ ﴿٧٠﴾

But when he saw their hands not reaching towards it, he became suspicious of them and started to fear them.

(*al-Hud* 11:70)

The mother of *Sayyidina* Musa ﷺ, is a powerful example shown to us. When Allah ﷻ told her to put her baby Musa ﷺ in the river, she became sad and afraid. Allah ﷻ reassured her, acknowledging it is natural to feel these emotions:

وَلَا تَخَافِى وَلَا تَحْزَنِىٓ ۖ إِنَّا رَآدُّوهُ إِلَيْكِ وَجَاعِلُوهُ مِنَ ٱلْمُرْسَلِينَ

And do not fear, nor be sad. We will return him to you, and will make him one of the Messengers.

(*al-Qasas* 28:7)

Feeling fear can be a way we are tested as we learn in several places in the Qur'an. For example in Surah *al-Baqarah* we are told:

وَلَنَبْلُوَنَّكُم بِشَىْءٍ مِّنَ ٱلْخَوْفِ وَٱلْجُوعِ وَنَقْصٍ مِّنَ ٱلْأَمْوَٰلِ وَٱلْأَنفُسِ وَٱلثَّمَرَٰتِ ۗ وَبَشِّرِ ٱلصَّٰبِرِينَ ﴿١٥٥﴾
ٱلَّذِينَ إِذَآ أَصَٰبَتْهُم مُّصِيبَةٌ قَالُوٓا۟ إِنَّا لِلَّهِ وَإِنَّآ إِلَيْهِ رَٰجِعُونَ ﴿١٥٦﴾

And We will surely test you with something of fear and hunger and a loss of wealth and lives and fruits, but give good tidings to the patient, who, when disaster strikes them, say, "Indeed we belong to Allāh, and indeed to Him we will return."

(*al-Baqarah* 2:155-156)

Ibn Kathir comments that some of our tests are visible outwardly like hunger and fear, while others are inward tests of our emotions, such as losing friends or loved ones to death. In the following narration, we find the attitude to develop when tested with fear. Umm Salamah ﵂ reported: I heard the Messenger of Allah ﷺ saying, "When a person suffers from a calamity and utters: We belong to Allah and to Him we shall return. O Allah! Compensate me in my affliction, recompense my loss and give me something better in exchange for it, then Allah surely compensates him with reward and a better substitute." Umm Salamah ﵂ said: "When Abu Salamah ﵁ died, I repeated the same supplication as the Messenger of Allah ﷺ had commanded me (to do). So Allah bestowed upon me a better substitute than him (I was married to Muhammad, the Messenger of Allah ﷺ)". (Riyad as-Salihin 921)

Allah ﷻ is with us

Turning to the *Seerah* we find more advice on how to tackle fear. In the famous story of the *Hijrah*, our beloved Prophet ﷺ left Makkah to undertake the migration journey to Madinah with *Sayyidina* Abu Bakr ﵁. When they took shelter in the cave and the disbelievers were pursuing them, Abu Bakr al-Siddiq ﵁ saw their feet at the opening of the cave and was afraid. He looked at *Rasul Allah* ﷺ and said to him 'Ya *Rasul Allah* ﷺ if they look down they will see us' and the Prophet ﷺ responded ' لَا تَحْزَنْ, don't be sad, إِنَّ ٱللَّهَ مَعَنَا. Allah is with us.'

A similar incident is found in an episode of *Sayyidina* Musa's life. In the most fearful moment when Pharaoh and his soldiers were furiously chasing *Sayyidina* Musa ﵇ and the strong believers, they felt afraid in spite of their unshakeable faith. When they saw the Pharaoh and his soldiers behind them, Allah ﷻ tells us their response:

إِنَّا لَمُدْرَكُونَ *They told him, they're going to catch us. And they felt afraid. And he said,*

قَالَ كَلَّآ إِنَّ مَعِىَ رَبِّى سَيَهْدِينِ

He said: By no means; Surely Allah is with me;
He will show me a way out.

(*ash-Shuara* 26:62).

Sayyidina Musa ﵇ reassured his followers, the same way *Rasul Allah* ﷺ reassured Abu Bakr al-Siddiq ﵁.

Feeling sad, feeling anxious, down, or restless is absolutely normal and natural. What should we do to address these feelings? There are two things we can put into practise: the first is the guidance from the Qur'an and the second is seeking suitable medical help.

There is an amazing verse in the Qur'an that provides an outline of what should be our initial action point:

اَلَا بِذِكْرِ اللّٰهِ تَطْمَئِنُّ الْقُلُوْبُ

Verily, by the remembrance of Allah, hearts will feel serene.

(*al-Ra'ad* 13:28)

Allah ﷻ is telling us our hearts will feel calm and the fear will leave when we remember Him. This is something that comes with time and habit, by constantly being in the remembrance of Allah. Furthermore, only being conscious of Allah ﷻ when we feel sad is not what is meant here, rather it is remembering Allah ﷻ, in the way that our Prophet ﷺ taught us, through the morning and evening *adhkar*-remembrance, reading a portion of Qur'an daily, even one page, or more or less as long as it's part of our daily routine. The point here is that remembrance needs to be built into our day.

Then, when we turn to Allah ﷻ, seeking refuge, we will find the remedy by Allah's ﷻ permission. In one hadith of *Rasul Allah* ﷺ, he taught us how to fight or avoid worries, by reciting the *as-salawat al-nabi alayhi salatu was-salam*. And the famous hadith of *Sayyidina* Ubay ﷻ, when he was talking to *Rasul Allah* ﷺ, and he asked 'how much of my time should I do *salawat*-send blessings to you, is it one-fourth, one-third, or should I spend all my time?' And he ﷺ replied تُكْفَى هَمَّكَ. then you will have nothing to worry about', indicating the more *salawat* we send on the Prophet ﷺ the less fear we will experience.

The second action we can take immediately after is to seek practical help. If our feelings become overwhelming in a way that it is restricting our life, as in we cannot function, serve, do our work, or perform our role as a mother or father, then we need to seek help, whether it's counselling or medication. This is clearly what our *deen* tells us, that we should take the means, نَأخُذ بِالْأَسْبَابِ, but we don't believe that the medicine or the counsellor alone is going to heal. We believe Allah ﷻ is the healer. Allah ﷻ will make the medicine or the counselling sessions work and be a *means* to help resolve the feelings.

As *Sayyidina Ibrahim* ﷺ said,

وَإِذَا مَرِضْتُ فَهُوَ يَشْفِينِ

When I get sick, He, Allah, will cure me.

(*ash-Shuara* 26:80)

What have we learnt from these verses and narrations? These feelings we experience are normal and natural. If we are overtaken by them, and they affect our daily life in a major way, then we need to get help. The primary remedy is in the Qur'an: whenever we feel afraid, we should pick up the Qur'an and read a verse. Even if we don't know the meaning, we should preserve and keep reading as Allah ﷻ will put the feeling of serenity in our heart. Allah ﷻ is *As-Salam* – He is peace, He has peace and He's the source of peace. If we want to feel peaceful we need to go to the source of peace: Allah ﷻ.

Points to reflect on:

- Our emotions are recognised in the Qur'an so we should acknowledge people's feelings and not dismiss them.
- Feelings of fear and anxiety can be a way we are tested, and we accept that we can't live this life without being tested.
- A test is truly a test if it takes us away from Allah ﷻ, but if the test gets us closer to Allah ﷻ it is a bounty.
- When we experience fear or anxiety, we should create the habit of turning to the Qur'an and *salah* without delay.
- We can acquaint ourselves with the way various prophets handled fear and take inspiration from their experience.
- Allah ﷻ is always with us in every situation as long as we are in regular remembrance of Him.
- Seeking medical help is advisable if difficult and negative feelings begin to take over our lives.

وَالضُّحَىٰ ۝ وَاللَّيْلِ إِذَا سَجَىٰ ۝ مَا وَدَّعَكَ رَبُّكَ وَمَا قَلَىٰ ۝ وَلَلْآخِرَةُ خَيْرٌ لَكَ
مِنَ الْأُولَىٰ ۝ وَلَسَوْفَ يُعْطِيكَ رَبُّكَ فَتَرْضَىٰ ۝ أَلَمْ يَجِدْكَ يَتِيمًا فَآوَىٰ ۝
وَوَجَدَكَ ضَالًّا فَهَدَىٰ ۝ وَوَجَدَكَ عَائِلًا فَأَغْنَىٰ ۝ فَأَمَّا الْيَتِيمَ فَلَا تَقْهَرْ ۝ وَأَمَّا
السَّائِلَ فَلَا تَنْهَرْ ۝ وَأَمَّا بِنِعْمَةِ رَبِّكَ فَحَدِّثْ ۝

By the morning brightness And the night as it settles. Your Lord did not abandon you, nor is He displeased. The Hereafter is better for you than the First. And your Lord will give you, and you will be satisfied. Did He not find you orphaned, and He sheltered you? And found you wandering, and He guided you? And found you in need, and He enriched you? Therefore, do not mistreat the orphan. Nor snub the seeker. But proclaim the blessings of your Lord.

(*al-Ḍuḥā* 93:1-11)

Chapter 26

DOES THE QUR'AN TALK ABOUT ILLNESS?

Our health is one of the most precious parts of our life. Yet this is tested when we suffer from an illness or a disease, be that a common flu or something more serious. Does Allah ﷻ address illness and wellbeing in the Qur'an, and if so, what does He say? It is interesting to find that the concept of illness in the Qur'an is framed in two ways physical illness and the internal, spiritual diseases.

Allah's Will and physical illness

Sayyidina Ibrahim's ﷺ story are some of the most beautiful verses in the Qur'an, where he is explaining to his people and teaching them who Allah ﷻ is:

ٱلَّذِى خَلَقَنِى فَهُوَ يَهْدِينِ

(He) who created me. It is He who guides me;

وَٱلَّذِى هُوَ يُطْعِمُنِى وَيَسْقِينِ

He who gives me food and drink.

وَإِذَا مَرِضْتُ فَهُوَ يَشْفِينِ

And when I get sick, He heals me.

(*ash-Shuara* 26: 78-80).

We can take vital lessons from the way the Qur'an talks about physical illness and how we should approach it. The first thing we need to constantly remember is it is Allah ﷻ who allowed it to happen. Then we need to seek help by going to see a physician to get treatment; it could be that surgery is needed, or medication. When we receive the treatment and are cured and recovered, we need to remember that Allah ﷻ put the cure in the hand of the surgeon or nurse. When we take medication, we know this alone is not responsible for the cure – it only works by the Will of Allah. When Allah ﷻ permits the medication to work, then the person is healed, even for something as simple as taking a painkiller for a headache.

Another mention Allah ﷻ makes about sickness is in relation to a person who may be ill or on a journey أَوْ عَلَىٰ سَفَرٍ وَإِن كُنتُم مَّرْضَىٰٓ. (*al-Nisa* 4: 43).

In this circumstance, Allah ﷻ gives permission to do wudu in a limited way as long as it's not harmful, and if this is not possible, then *tayammum*[1] is acceptable.[2]

Physical illness is something we are tested with, some people suffer more, some less. The best way to respond to it is to have gratitude and patience when we undergo any ill health, and try to draw closer to Allah ﷻ even though this may be a very trying time.

Disease of the Heart

The second way illness is addressed in the Qur'an is the sickness of the heart. Allah ﷻ repeats this in many *surahs*. In *Surah al-Baqarah* -The Cow, those lying about their belief, who deceive themselves and cause corruption are being addressed:

فِى قُلُوبِهِم مَّرَضٌ فَزَادَهُمُ ٱللَّهُ مَرَضًا

There is a disease in their hearts, to which Allah ﷻ has added more: agonising torment awaits them for their persistent lying.

(*al-Baqarah* 2:10)

The disease of the heart is when the heart persistently doesn't see truth as truth, and does not see falsehood as falsehood. It alternates or changes, as there are two forces at play in that heart.

The Prophet ﷺ said: "There are two impulses in the soul, one from an angel which calls towards good and confirms truth; whoever finds this let him know it is from God and praise Him. Another impulse comes from the enemy which leads to doubt and denies truth and forbids good; whoever finds this, let him seek refuge in God from the accursed devil." Then he recited the verse: "*Satan threatens you with poverty and orders you to fahshah (immorality)*" (*al-Baqarah* 2:268) (At-Tirmidhi).

As *Rasul Allah* ﷺ said, لَمَّتَان, the heart has two forces: 'لَمَّةُ الْمَلِك وَ لَمَّةُ الشَّيْطَان: one from the angel and one from *Shaytan*'. When we want to do something and we know that this thing is not pleasing to Allah, there are two voices

2 Tayammum is a dry ablution using clean Earth when water is unavailable.

inside us competing, one saying *don't do it, it's not pleasing to Allah* and the other voice saying *it's okay, it's only a one-off; Allah will forgive you*, and any other justification used to convince us. This is when we experience a heart that is not dead, but unwell. How sick the heart is depends on which force wins. If the good impulse can defeat the whispers of *shaytan*, then the disease is averted and our heart continues to be healthy.

Allah ﷻ mentioned فِى قُلُوبِهِم مَّرَضٌ – '*the sick at heart*' as a caution when He addressed the wives of *Rasul Allah* ﷺ in the chapter *al-Ahzab*, The Confederate.

يَٰنِسَآءَ ٱلنَّبِىِّ لَسْتُنَّ كَأَحَدٍ مِّنَ ٱلنِّسَآءِ ۚ إِنِ ٱتَّقَيْتُنَّ فَلَا تَخْضَعْنَ بِٱلْقَوْلِ فَيَطْمَعَ
ٱلَّذِى فِى قَلْبِهِۦ مَرَضٌ وَقُلْنَ قَوْلًا مَّعْرُوفًا ۝

O Wives of the Prophet, you are not like any other woman. If you are truly mindful of God, do not speak too softly in case the sick at heart should lust after you, but speak in an appropriate manner;

(*al-Azhab* 33:32)

This is a caution to protect the wives of *Rasul Allah* ﷺ from anyone who may have had a disease in the heart and may interpret what is said in a way that feeds their desires. Allah ﷻ knows what we feel and knows what affects us.

In *Surah al-Tawbah*, Allah ﷻ mentions the sick heart again, this time in relation to when a verse of the Qur'an was revealed and the effect it had on two groups of people in Madinah:

وَإِذَا مَآ أُنزِلَتْ سُورَةٌ فَمِنْهُم مَّن يَقُولُ أَيُّكُمْ زَادَتْهُ هَٰذِهِۦٓ إِيمَٰنًا ۚ فَأَمَّا ٱلَّذِينَ
ءَامَنُوا۟ فَزَادَتْهُمْ إِيمَٰنًا وَهُمْ يَسْتَبْشِرُونَ ۝
وَأَمَّا ٱلَّذِينَ فِى قُلُوبِهِم مَّرَضٌ فَزَادَتْهُمْ رِجْسًا إِلَىٰ رِجْسِهِمْ وَمَاتُوا۟ وَهُمْ كَٰفِرُونَ ۝

When a surah is revealed, some [hypocrites] say, 'Have any of you been strengthened in faith by it?' It certainly does strengthen the faith of those who believe and they rejoice, but, as for the perverse at heart, each new surah adds further to their perversity. They die disbelieving.

(*al-Tawbah* 9:124-125)

The verse tells us the difference between the genuine believers who are happy to receive revelation, in contrast to those who have a sickness in their heart. When a verse is revealed, their heart increases in, رِجْسًا meaning 'filth' or 'more doubt'.

In relation to ourselves, we can look inwards and ask ourselves: *When I read the Qur'an, when I listen to a verse, what does it do to me? When I read the Qur'an, where do I stand; am I the person who gets closer to Allah ﷻ and increases in faith; or am I going to have more doubt? If I'm not convinced and resist, is there a disease in my heart?*

Allah ﷻ in subtle ways gives us clues to look internally and look at the condition of our hearts.

The best cure for diseases of the heart

One of the best cures for the diseases of the heart is in the Qur'an itself, in *Surah al-Isra*, Allah ﷻ tells us:

وَنُنَزِّلُ مِنَ ٱلْقُرْءَانِ مَا هُوَ شِفَآءٌ وَرَحْمَةٌ لِّلْمُؤْمِنِينَ ۙ وَلَا يَزِيدُ ٱلظَّٰلِمِينَ إِلَّا خَسَارًا ۝

We send down the Quran as healing and mercy to those who believe; as for those who disbelieve, it only increases their loss.

(*al-Isra* 17:82)

What does Allah ﷻ, expect from us? The internal diseases of the heart are the most important in terms of examining ourselves every day and asking the following questions: *Is my heart sick? Do I have a disease of the heart? Do I have jealousy or anger? Do I have arrogance?* Sometimes, we don't know our own state, but we can notice our response to reading the Qur'an: is it argumentative or accepting? If we experience negativity, we need to seek the help of Allah ﷻ to cure us:

اللهمّ آتِ نفسي تقواها وزكّها أنت خيرُ من زكّاها ۝

O Allah, Grant me the sense of piety and purify my soul as You are the best to purify it. Amīn (*Riyad as-Salihin* 1479).

May Allah ﷻ cure our physical and spiritual illnesses and make the Qur'an a healing for our hearts and protect us from the diseases that distance us from Him. May He purify our hearts from every spiritual malady. Amīn.

Points to reflect on:

- When we get ill, we need to remember everything happens through Allah's ﷻ permission only, this helps us to accept His Will and seek His help.
- Any illness is an opportunity to practise patience and steadfastness, and to draw closer to Allah ﷻ through the experience.
- Physical illness is cured by physicians only if Allah ﷻ Wills. How do we react when we are tested with an illness; acceptance or complaining?
- Diseases of the heart like hypocrisy, suspicion, or pride are more dangerous than physical ones, because they affect our life on Earth and our hereafter.
- Taking daily account of the diseases of our heart should be inbuilt in our routine the way physical activity is scheduled for our body's wellbeing. Both require attention.
- Reading and reflecting on the Qur'an regularly helps cleanse the heart and restore spiritual well-being.

الم ۝ أَحَسِبَ النَّاسُ أَنْ يُتْرَكُوا أَنْ يَقُولُوا آمَنَّا وَهُمْ لَا يُفْتَنُونَ ۝ وَلَقَدْ فَتَنَّا
الَّذِينَ مِنْ قَبْلِهِمْ ۖ فَلَيَعْلَمَنَّ اللَّهُ الَّذِينَ صَدَقُوا وَلَيَعْلَمَنَّ الْكَاذِبِينَ ۝
أَمْ حَسِبَ الَّذِينَ يَعْمَلُونَ السَّيِّئَاتِ أَنْ يَسْبِقُونَا ۚ سَاءَ مَا يَحْكُمُونَ ۝ مَنْ كَانَ
يَرْجُو لِقَاءَ اللَّهِ فَإِنَّ أَجَلَ اللَّهِ لَآتٍ ۚ وَهُوَ السَّمِيعُ الْعَلِيمُ ۝ وَمَنْ جَاهَدَ فَإِنَّمَا
يُجَاهِدُ لِنَفْسِهِ ۚ إِنَّ اللَّهَ لَغَنِيٌّ عَنِ الْعَالَمِينَ ۝ وَالَّذِينَ آمَنُوا وَعَمِلُوا الصَّالِحَاتِ
لَنُكَفِّرَنَّ عَنْهُمْ سَيِّئَاتِهِمْ وَلَنَجْزِيَنَّهُمْ أَحْسَنَ الَّذِي كَانُوا يَعْمَلُونَ ۝

Alif, Lām, Mīm. Do people think they will be left alone to say, "We believe," without being tested? We tested those before them. Allah certainly knows those who are thankful, and He certainly knows the liars. Or do those who commit bad deeds think they can outdo us? Terrible is their judgment! Whoever looks forward to the meeting with Allah—Allah's appointed time is coming. He is the Hearing, the Knowing. Whoever strives, strives only for himself. Allah is beyond the need of the worlds. Those who believe and do good works: We will remit their sins, and We will reward them according to the best of what they used to do.

(*al-ʿAnkabūt* 29:1-7)

Chapter 27

DOES THE QUR'AN DESCRIBE DEATH?

One of the absolute truths and only certainty is that we're going to die and meet Allah ﷻ. This certainty has a central place in the Qur'an, which covers death and dying from many angles. In this chapter we are going to reflect on what the Qur'an says about the moment of our death. In the following chapter we will look at what happens when a person dies.

In a powerful verse which depicts the moment death arrives, Allah ﷻ says in *Surah Qaf*:

وَجَآءَتْ سَكْرَةُ ٱلْمَوْتِ بِٱلْحَقِّ ۖ ذَٰلِكَ مَا كُنتَ مِنْهُ تَحِيدُ

Death throes will bring the truth with it: This is what you tried to escape. (*Qaf* 50:19)

When Allah ﷻ says, وَجَآءَتْ سَكْرَةُ ٱلْمَوْتِ , the word سَكْرَةُ comes from *sakara,* which means intoxication, so the moment of dying is likened to someone who is intoxicated. He or she does not know what is going on around them externally. However internally it is a different experience. Allah ﷻ used وَجَاءَتْ, 'came', meaning 'the moment of intoxication came and brought the truth: بالحق. – *al haqq*'. Many commentators agree this verse is stating how death brings the truth. Human beings tend to avoid this reality, running away from it and thinking it will always happen to someone else. Even though we witness death regularly, we forget that we too will die.

Some of us may have witnessed a person dying and noticed how, when they are taking their last breaths, they look into the distance, but we are unaware of what they are looking at. Whilst they hear us, only Allah ﷻ knows what they are actually conscious of. Allah ﷻ is the closest as He says in the previous *ayaat*:

We created humans, and know exactly what their desires urge them to do; in fact We are closer to that human being than their jugular vein. When the two recording angels, one sitting on their right and the other on their left, record. Not a word they speak goes unrecorded by a vigilant observer. (*Qaf* 50:16-18).

During our lifetime the angels record everything we say and do, even though Allah's ﷻ knowledge encompasses everything. On the Day of Judgement, we will have no way to deny what we have done or said because Allah ﷻ will show us our record. Yet His mercy for us is shown in a hadith of *Rasul Allah* ﷺ which tells us of the two angels that write our records; the one on the right recording our good deeds, and that on the left recording our sin. The angel on the left waits for six hours if a sin is committed, in the hope that the person who committed that sin will repent and therefore it won't be recorded. It is only after this that a bad deed is recorded.

Rasul Allah's ﷺ own moment of death serves as a powerful reminder to us, as described by *Sayyidah* Aisha ﵂. She said when the intoxicating moment of death came to him ﷺ, he put his hand in a wooden container of water and wiped his forehead saying: لا إله إلا الله إن للموت لسكرات '*There is none worthy of worship but Allāh, surely death has agonies*'. At this point the Angel of death ﵇ came to him and gave him the choice: 'Do you want to stay here or do you want to be with the *Rafiq Al-Ala*, the High Companion?' *Rasul Allah* ﷺ replied بِالرَّفِيْقِ الْأَعْلٰى, 'With the Highest Companion' and then he passed away.

We need to reflect on *Rasul Allah's* ﷺ death. He, who was the devoted servant of Allah, the one who is the key, the first one who is going to open *Jannah*, the one whose sins were all forgiven, felt the pains of death. What do we expect to face?

In one hadith we learn what happens when the believer's soul leaves the body. For the righteous person, it will leave very quickly and softly. The opposite is experienced by the soul that is not righteous. A verse in *Surah al-Waqiah* describes this moment:

فَلَوْلَا إِذَا بَلَغَتِ الْحُلْقُومَ ۝ وَأَنتُمْ حِينَئِذٍ تَنظُرُونَ ۝
وَنَحْنُ أَقْرَبُ إِلَيْهِ مِنكُمْ وَلَٰكِن لَّا تُبْصِرُونَ ۝

So when it has reached the throat. While you are looking on. We are closer to it than you are, but you cannot see.

(*al-Wāqi'ah* 56:83-85)

Here, the soul is described as reaching the throat-*al-hulqoom*. The onlookers are not aware of all that is going on, as it is only Allah ﷻ who is the closest and aware.

Why did Allah ﷻ put this level of detail in the Qur'an? These moments serve to remind us that one day we will experience the pain of dying. The question for all of us is: are we ready? If this happens today, or tomorrow, are we ready to go and meet Allah ﷻ? We need to be ready for this inevitability. Allah ﷻ described in several places in the Qur'an what being ready means:

وَالَّذِينَ آمَنُوا وَعَمِلُوا الصَّالِحَاتِ أُولَٰئِكَ أَصْحَابُ الْجَنَّةِ ۖ هُمْ فِيهَا خَالِدُونَ

And those who have believed and done righteous deeds are the companions of Paradise; they will abide therein eternally.

(al-Baqarah 2:82)

Through our intentions, we can prepare by transforming everything in our daily lives into an act of worship to Allah ﷻ. We see in the example of *Sayyidina* Bilal ؓ, his contented state when he was dying as he said, غدًا نلقى الأحبّة محمّدًا وصحبه. 'Finally, tomorrow, I am going to go and meet Muhammad ﷺ and his companions'. As Bilal ؓ spent all his life in the obedience of Allah ﷻ, he knew his destination.

May Allah ﷻ help us learn and be ready with a good record for that moment. May Allah ﷻ make that moment easy for us and may He shower His mercy on us and on everyone who has passed away before us. Ya Rabbi Amīn.

Points to reflect on:

- Regardless of our appearance, status or wealth, we will each taste death and cannot escape from it.
- The way we live our lives can affect the way we experience our last moments. Thinking about this should make our decisions and actions more focused on the *akhirah*.
- Death should be our motivator to become better believers in the sight of Allah ﷻ.
- We need to be aware that Allah ﷻ is the only One who knows when we will die, as He is the One who has already ordained it.
- Allah ﷻ gives us life and death, and does not need anything from us. However, we are in constant need of Him.
- We should ask Allah ﷻ to take our soul when we are closest to Him, in the best state of worship and with a pure heart.

وَأَنفِقُوا۟ مِن مَّا رَزَقْنَـٰكُم مِّن قَبْلِ أَن يَأْتِىَ أَحَدَكُمُ ٱلْمَوْتُ فَيَقُولَ رَبِّ لَوْلَآ
أَخَّرْتَنِىٓ إِلَىٰٓ أَجَلٍ قَرِيبٍ فَأَصَّدَّقَ وَأَكُن مِّنَ ٱلصَّـٰلِحِينَ ﴿١٠﴾
وَلَن يُؤَخِّرَ ٱللَّهُ نَفْسًا إِذَا جَآءَ أَجَلُهَا ۚ وَٱللَّهُ خَبِيرٌۢ بِمَا تَعْمَلُونَ ﴿١١﴾

Give out of what We have provided for you, before death comes to one of you and he says, 'My Lord, if You would only reprieve me for a little while, I would give in charity and become one of the righteous.' God does not reprieve a soul when its turn comes: God is fully aware of what you do.

(*al-Munafiqoon* 63:10-11)

Chapter 28

WHAT DOES THE QUR'AN SAY ABOUT ACCOUNTABILITY?

While we live our lives in this world, we make many choices about what we do and what we avoid. Do the choices we make and the things we do just stay in this world when it is time for us to die? What does the Qur'an say about this? Allah ﷻ makes it clear in the Qur'an that everything we do on Earth will come with us, there will be no separation between us and our deeds. On the Day of Judgement, our actions are going to come in front of us; each day we lived on Earth will be presented to us; moment by moment.

Our Book of Deeds

Allah ﷻ made it clear in the Qur'an in *Surah al-Isra*, The Night Journey:

وَكُلَّ إِنسَـٰنٍ أَلْزَمْنَـٰهُ طَـٰٓئِرَهُۥ فِى عُنُقِهِۦ ۖ وَنُخْرِجُ لَهُۥ يَوْمَ ٱلْقِيَـٰمَةِ كِتَـٰبًا يَلْقَىٰهُ مَنشُورًا ۝ ٱقْرَأْ كِتَـٰبَكَ كَفَىٰ بِنَفْسِكَ ٱلْيَوْمَ عَلَيْكَ حَسِيبًا ۝

We have bound each human being's destiny to his neck. On the Day of Resurrection, We shall bring out a record for each of them, which they will find spread wide open, 'Read your record. Today your own soul is enough to calculate your account.'

(*Bani Isra'il* 17:13-14)

If we look at the words Allah ﷻ uses 'إِنسَـٰنٍ أَلْزَمْنَـٰهُ طَـٰٓئِرَهُۥ' the deeds are likened to birds fastened to our necks because deeds, like birds, are fleeting and fly away from our memory. We tend to forget what we've done last week, last month, or last year. However, Allah ﷻ is telling us these deeds are attached to our neck and they will not leave us. On the Day of Judgement, Allah ﷻ will bring it forth in a book and present it to us. In *Surah al-Kahf* Allah ﷻ details an encounter of a person's reaction when they receive their book:

وَوُضِعَ ٱلْكِتَـٰبُ فَتَرَى ٱلْمُجْرِمِينَ مُشْفِقِينَ مِمَّا فِيهِ وَيَقُولُونَ يَـٰوَيْلَتَنَا مَالِ هَـٰذَا ٱلْكِتَـٰبِ لَا يُغَادِرُ صَغِيرَةً وَلَا كَبِيرَةً إِلَّآ أَحْصَىٰهَا ۚ وَوَجَدُوا۟ مَا عَمِلُوا۟ حَاضِرًا ۗ وَلَا يَظْلِمُ رَبُّكَ أَحَدًا

The record of their deeds will be laid open and you will see the guilty, dismayed at what they contain, saying, 'Woe to us! What a record this is! It does not leave any deed, small or large, unaccounted for!'

They will find everything they ever did laid in front of them: your Lord will not be unjust to anyone.

(*al-Kahf* 18:49)

A person receiving their record on the Day of Judgement will comment that this book does not leave anything, significant or trivial out; nothing is forgotten. What we say and do is not only being recorded, but each individual will be responsible for explaining their actions or being rewarded for what they did. The concept of accountability in Islam is one that reinforces justice, as nobody will be wronged in the slightest. Nor, as we read in *Surah al-Fatir*, is anyone responsible for another's actions:

وَلَا تَزِرُ وَازِرَةٌ وِزْرَ أُخْرَىٰ

No soul will carry the burden of the others.

(*al-Fatir* 35:18).

If we make a mistake, sometimes we face the result in this *dunya*. Other times if we don't see the effect in the *dunya*, that does not mean Allah ﷻ is unaware, or that it's not recorded. On the contrary, as we find in *Surah Maryam*:

وَمَا كَانَ رَبُّكَ نَسِيًّا

Your Lord never forgets.

(*Maryam* 19:64)

Receiving our book

فَأَمَّا مَنْ أُوتِىَ كِتَـٰبَهُۥ بِيَمِينِهِۦ فَيَقُولُ هَآؤُمُ ٱقْرَءُوا۟ كِتَـٰبِيَهْ ۝ إِنِّى ظَنَنتُ أَنِّى
مُلَـٰقٍ حِسَابِيَهْ ۝ فَهُوَ فِى عِيشَةٍ رَّاضِيَةٍ ۝ فِى جَنَّةٍ عَالِيَةٍ ۝
قُطُوفُهَا دَانِيَةٌ ۝ كُلُوا۟ وَٱشْرَبُوا۟ هَنِيٓـًٔا بِمَآ أَسْلَفْتُمْ فِى ٱلْأَيَّامِ ٱلْخَالِيَةِ ۝ وَأَمَّا
مَنْ أُوتِىَ كِتَـٰبَهُۥ بِشِمَالِهِۦ فَيَقُولُ يَـٰلَيْتَنِى لَمْ أُوتَ كِتَـٰبِيَهْ ۝ وَلَمْ أَدْرِ مَا
حِسَابِيَهْ ۝ يَـٰلَيْتَهَا كَانَتِ ٱلْقَاضِيَةَ ۝ مَآ أَغْنَىٰ عَنِّى مَالِيَهْ ۜ ۝ هَلَكَ عَنِّى
سُلْطَـٰنِيَهْ ۝

So as for he who is given his record in his right hand, he will say, "Here, read my record! Indeed, I was certain that I would be meeting my account." So he will be in a pleasant life-In an elevated garden, Its [fruit] to be picked hanging near. [They will be told], "Eat and drink in satisfaction for what you put forth in the days past." But as for he who is given his record in his left hand, he will say, "Oh, I wish I had not been given my record and had not known what is my account. I wish it [i.e., my death] had been the decisive one. My wealth has not availed me. Gone from me is my authority."

(*al-Haaqqah* 69:19-29)

In *Surah al-Haaqqah* – The Reality, we are shown the scene on the Day of Judgement when we will be invited to read our book, Allah ﷻ says:

يَوْمَئِذٍ تُعْرَضُونَ لَا تَخْفَىٰ مِنكُمْ خَافِيَةٌ ۝

On that Day you will be brought to judgement and none of your secrets will remain hidden.

(*al-Haaqqah* 69:18)

Then we are shown how someone reacts when they receive their book in their right hand:

. إِنِّي ظَنَنتُ أَنِّي مُلَاقٍ حِسَابِيَهْ

Surely, I knew that I shall meet my account.

(*al-Haaqqah* 69:20)

This person says they were prepared. They would have lived their life consistently aware of Allah's ﷻ limits and inevitable accountability, therefore taking full responsibility for their actions. This person who prepares for the *akhirah*, scrutinises every act in their life as a means for eternal happiness in the hereafter. Allah ﷻ then describes the eternal life they will be content with:

فَهُوَ فِى عِيشَةٍ رَّاضِيَةٍ

He or she will have a life of pleasure.

(*al-Haaqqah* 69:21)

The opposite is also true. The one who did not take responsibility or pay attention to their *akhirah*, will experience an opposite fate of regret. They will say: يَٰلَيۡتَنِي لَمۡ أُوتَ كِتَٰبِيَهۡ *I wish the book was not given to me* (*al-Haaqqah* 69:25). When they see the result of their life, they're going to beg Allah ﷻ to send them back. The scene is described in detail to us in *Surah al-Muminun* – The Believers:

حَتَّىٰٓ إِذَا جَآءَ أَحَدَهُمُ ٱلۡمَوۡتُ قَالَ رَبِّ ٱرۡجِعُونِ ۝ لَعَلِّيٓ أَعۡمَلُ صَٰلِحٗا فِيمَا تَرَكۡتُۚ كَلَّآۚ إِنَّهَا كَلِمَةٌ هُوَ قَآئِلُهَاۖ وَمِن وَرَآئِهِم بَرۡزَخٌ إِلَىٰ يَوۡمِ يُبۡعَثُونَ ۝

When death comes to one of them, he cries, 'My Lord, let me return so as to make amends for the things I neglected.' Never! This will not go beyond his words: a barrier stands behind such people until the very Day they are resurrected.

(*al-Muminun* 23: 99-100)

Purpose and accountability

Here and now, we have time in this life to fulfil our purpose, which is to represent Allah ﷻ (as *Khalifa*) and worship Him, as we discussed in chapter one. At the same time, we will have to face the consequences for any good or bad we do during our life. What Allah ﷻ wants from us is to obey Him ﷻ and follow in the footsteps of our *Rasul Allah* ﷺ. Allah ﷻ has clearly detailed what is lawful and good for us, and everything that is not good for us *haram* – unlawful.

وَيُحِلُّ لَهُمُ الطَّيِّبَاتِ وَيُحَرِّمُ عَلَيْهِمُ الْخَبَائِثَ

And [He] allows for them all good things, and prohibits for them wickedness

(*al-A'rāf* 7:157)

Let's reflect and contemplate while we still are alive. We can start by thinking about our habits, are these going to be a source of joy or regret for us on the Day of Judgement? Can we change? Yes, of course, there is always the option to change and Allah ﷻ will make things easy. Anytime we want to get closer to Allah ﷻ, He will facilitate it. If we take the initiative, He will help us with the rest.

May Allah ﷻ make us all from the people, who will be given their book in their right hand. May we be amongst those who will be happy and look forward to our place in *Jannah*. Ya Rabbi Amīn.

Points to reflect on

- Allah ﷻ is All Knowing, All Seeing, All Hearing of everything we do and say. The five *salah* help us recall this reality.
- We will be held accountable for our deeds and will be asked about our life and how we spent it.
- We are in control of what is written in our book of deeds, as long as we can control our *nafs*.
- We can work to fill our book with good deeds, repent from our sins and ask Allah ﷻ to cover all our mistakes out of His mercy.
- We have the opportunity now to make sure our book is not full of sins and cause us shame. We know that on the Day of Judgement those who are regretful will ask to come back to this world and will want to rewrite their deeds. May we not be of these people.
- The advice from 'Umar ibn Khattab ؓ can help us in preparation for being held accountable. He said: "Hold yourself accountable before you are held accountable and weigh your deeds before they are weighed for you".
- How will we feel to read our book in front of Allah ﷻ? We have time now to repent and invest in all that pleases *Al-Haseeb* – The Reckoner, The One Who holds account.

وَلِلَّهِ مَا فِي السَّمَاوَاتِ وَمَا فِي الْأَرْضِ لِيَجْزِيَ الَّذِينَ أَسَاءُوا بِمَا عَمِلُوا وَيَجْزِيَ الَّذِينَ أَحْسَنُوا بِالْحُسْنَى
الَّذِينَ يَجْتَنِبُونَ كَبَائِرَ الْإِثْمِ وَالْفَوَاحِشَ إِلَّا اللَّمَمَ ۚ إِنَّ رَبَّكَ وَاسِعُ الْمَغْفِرَةِ ۚ هُوَ أَعْلَمُ بِكُمْ إِذْ أَنْشَأَكُمْ مِنَ الْأَرْضِ وَإِذْ أَنْتُمْ أَجِنَّةٌ فِي بُطُونِ أُمَّهَاتِكُمْ ۖ فَلَا تُزَكُّوا أَنْفُسَكُمْ ۖ هُوَ أَعْلَمُ بِمَنِ اتَّقَىٰ

To Allah belongs whatever is in Heaven and whatever is on Earth. He will penalise those who commit evil according to their deeds. And He will reward those who do good with the best. Those who avoid major sins and indecencies—except what is slight—your Lord is of Vast Forgiveness. He knew you well, ever since He produced you from the Earth, and ever since you were embryos in your mothers' wombs. So do not acclaim your own virtue; He is fully aware of the righteous.

(*al-Najm* 53:31-32)

Chapter 29

DOES THE QUR'AN MENTION MEETING ALLAH ﷻ?

People have multiple goals and dreams. Some goals are for this world, others are focused on the hereafter. A believer recognises their time on this Earth is short, while the home in the hereafter is eternal. What does the Qur'an say about the best outcome for a believer? Allah ﷻ makes the answer to this question very clear in *Surah Yunus* – Jonah:

لِّلَّذِينَ أَحْسَنُوا۟ ٱلْحُسْنَىٰ وَزِيَادَةٌ ۖ وَلَا يَرْهَقُ وُجُوهَهُمْ قَتَرٌ وَلَا ذِلَّةٌ ۚ أُو۟لَٰٓئِكَ أَصْحَٰبُ ٱلْجَنَّةِ ۖ هُمْ فِيهَا خَٰلِدُونَ

For those who do good there will be an excellent reward and more besides. Neither gloom nor shame will cover their faces. These are the inhabitants of Paradise, abiding in it forever.

(*Yunus* 10:26).

The extra reward for the people of *Ihsan*

ٱلْحُسْنَىٰ *Al-husna* means goodness, indicating excellence and is also one of the names of *Jannah*. *'Ahsanu', is* the verb form from the same root as *al -husna*, referring to those who excelled in doing good with total sincerity. This *ayah* tells us that there is something extra وَزِيَادَةٌ, *ziyada* for those who acted beautifully with *ahsanu.*

What is this something extra? *Rasul Allah* ﷺ explained this in a remarkable hadith[1]. He ﷺ described that when the righteous people will enter *Jannah*, they will hear a voice saying Allah ﷻ wants to fulfil something that He promised you. And they will say what else will He give us? He made our scale heavy, and He is pleased with us and we are in *Jannah*. Then a veil is lifted, the details of which is from the knowledge of the unseen. When the veil is removed, the righteous will see Allah ﷻ; for those of *al-husna* this is *al-ziyadah,* the extra.

Scholars have questioned why the people of *ihsan* will be honoured with this. The answer is found in a famous hadith [2] when *Sayyidina* Jibrail ﷺ asked *Rasul Allah* ﷺ 'What is *ihsan*?' He ﷺ replied: 'أن تعبدَ اللهَ كأنّك تراه, To worship Allah ﷻ as if you are seeing Him. And even though you do not see Him, remember He's seeing you' (Sahih Muslim).

1See end of chapter for Hadith

2 See end of chapter for full Hadith

So the people of *ihsan*, who act and do things sincerely as if they are seeing Allah ﷻ and are conscious that He is seeing them, will have the veil removed. The righteous person's consciousness of Allah ﷻ in the *dunya*, will be rewarded by giving them the reality of seeing Him ﷻ in *Jannah*. Allah ﷻ also said:

وُجُوهٌ يَوْمَئِذٍ نَّاضِرَةٌ ۝ إِلَىٰ رَبِّهَا نَاظِرَةٌ

Some faces that day will be radiant, looking at their Lord.

(*al-Qiyama* 75:22-23)

Nādirah comes from *nadārah*, which means splendid, radiant, glowing, delighted with goodness and *Nādirah* refers to looking with the eyes; the believers will see their Lord with their very own eyes.

Further inspiration for the believer is given in the famous verse in *Surah al-Rahman*, where Allah ﷻ says:

هَلْ جَزَآءُ ٱلْإِحْسَٰنِ إِلَّا ٱلْإِحْسَٰنُ

What will be the reward of good but good?

(*al-Rahman* 55:60)

We are assured of the great rewards from Allah ﷻ for those who aspire to be the best. Allah ﷻ will never disappoint us. We can strive and aim to receive the best reward in *Jannah*, going beyond the first level in *Jannah* by aiming higher. In *dunya* we are ambitious and want the best, which is commendable, as long as we go about this in a way that pleases Allah ﷻ.

We can work hard to be the best in *akhirah* and ask Allah ﷻ for His help to reach *Jannat al-Firdous* and be the neighbour of *Rasul Allah* ﷺ. There, by the mercy and permission of Allah ﷻ,those excelling in righteousness will be looking at Allah ﷻ and Allah ﷻ will be looking at them, and there is nothing else a believer will want. In *Jannah* there will be no more pain, worry or sorrow forever. For this eternal خَٰلِدُونَ, reward, the only thing He wants from us is to believe in Him, work for Him, prioritise Him as number one in our life. When we work – is He pleased with what we do? When we speak or stay silent, are we pleasing Him? With every action we choose to do, or not do, our primary focus needs to be pleasing Allah ﷻ alone.

May Allah ﷻ make us all the people of *Jannah*. May Allah ﷻ make us among those لِّلَّذِينَ أَحْسَنُوا۟ ٱلْحُسْنَىٰ وَزِيَادَةٌ. Amīn.

Points to reflect on:

- What are our goals in life, are they for this world only or do they include *Jannah*?
- When we reflect on the meaning of *Ihsan* – to worship Allah ﷻ as if we see Him, we can examine our daily life and look for ways to improve our *ibaadah* and excel.
- Are we working sincerely to be amongst those who will be rewarded with *ziyādah* -extra reward? Or are we content with making minimum effort?
- Every choice we make reveals what we prioritise. The way we earn, interact with others, dress and speak are opportunities to please Allah ﷻ and seek His pleasure above all else.
- In this world the righteous believer is constantly aware of Allah ﷻ while He is not visible. In the hereafter, they will be rewarded with seeing Him because of their God consciousness on Earth.
- We should ask Allah ﷻ for the highest levels of *Jannah*. At the same time we strive sincerely to align our actions with all that pleases Him.
- Are we genuinely focused on seeking only Allah's ﷻ pleasure, or are we actually more concerned with the praise of people?
- When *Jannah* is our goal, then *dunya* is used as a vehicle to reach our destination.

بِسْمِ ٱللَّهِ ٱلرَّحْمَٰنِ ٱلرَّحِيمِ

طه ۝ مَا أَنْزَلْنَا عَلَيْكَ الْقُرْآنَ لِتَشْقَىٰ ۝ إِلَّا تَذْكِرَةً لِمَنْ يَخْشَىٰ ۝ تَنْزِيلًا مِمَّنْ
خَلَقَ الْأَرْضَ وَالسَّمَاوَاتِ الْعُلَى ۝ الرَّحْمَٰنُ عَلَى الْعَرْشِ اسْتَوَىٰ ۝ لَهُ مَا فِي
السَّمَاوَاتِ وَمَا فِي الْأَرْضِ وَمَا بَيْنَهُمَا وَمَا تَحْتَ الثَّرَىٰ ۝ وَإِنْ تَجْهَرْ بِالْقَوْلِ
فَإِنَّهُ يَعْلَمُ السِّرَّ وَأَخْفَى ۝ اللَّهُ لَا إِلَٰهَ إِلَّا هُوَ ۖ لَهُ الْأَسْمَاءُ الْحُسْنَىٰ

In the name of Allāh, the Merciful, the Mercifier.

Ṭā, Hā. We did not reveal the Qur'an to you to make you suffer. But only as a reminder for him who fears. A revelation from He Who created the Earth and the high heavens. The Mercy-Giver; on the Throne He settled. To Him belongs everything in the heavens, everything on Earth, everything between them, and everything beneath the soil. If you speak aloud—He knows the secret, and what is more hidden. Allah—there is no god except He. He has the Most Beautiful Names.

(*Ṭā Hā* 20:1-8)

Hadith references:

1. In a narration reported by Imam Ahmad, Suhayb ؓ stated that he heard the Messenger of Allah ﷺ recite لِّلَّذِينَ أَحْسَنُوا۟ ٱلْحُسْنَىٰ وَزِيَادَةٌ and then he said:

إذَا دَخَلَ أَهلُ الجَنَّةِ الجَنَّةَ وَأَهلُ النَّارِ النَّارَ نَادَى مُنَادٍ يَا أَهلَ الجَنَّةِ إنَّ لَكُم عِندَ اللهِ مَوعِدًا يُرِيدُ أن يُنجِزَكُمُوهُ . فَيَقُولُونَ وَمَا هُوَ أَلَم يُثَقِّلِ اللهُ مَوَازِينَنَا وَيُبَيِّض وُجُوهَنَا وَيُدخِلنَا الجَنَّةَ وَيُنجِنَا مِنَ النَّارِ قَالَ فَيَكشِفُ الحِجَابَ فَيَنظُرُونَ إلَيهِ فَوَاللهِ مَا أَعطَاهُمُ اللهُ شَيئًا أَحَبَّ إلَيهِم مِنَ النَّظَرِ إلَيهِ وَلا أَقَرَّ لأَعيُنِهِم

When the people of Paradise enter Paradise, a caller will say: "O people of Paradise, Allah has promised you something that He wishes to fulfill." They will reply: "What is it? Has He not made our scale heavy? Has He not made our faces white and delivered us from the Fire?" Allah will then remove the veil and they will see Him. By Allah, they have not been given anything dearer to them and more delightful than looking at Him.

2. Hadith of *Sayyidina* Jibrael ؑ

Narrated by 'Umar ibn al-Khattāb ؓ:

While we were sitting with the Messenger of Allah ﷺ one day, there appeared before us a man dressed in extremely white clothes and with very black hair. No signs of travel were visible on him, and none of us knew him.

He sat down next to the Prophet ﷺ, rested his knees against his knees, and placed his hands on his thighs. He said:

"O Muhammad, tell me about Islam."

The Messenger of Allah ﷺ said:

"Islam is to testify that there is no god but Allah and that Muhammad is the Messenger of Allah, to establish the prayer, to give zakat, to fast Ramadan, and to perform Hajj if you are able."

The man said: "You have spoken the truth."

We were amazed that he asked him and then confirmed his answer!

He then said: "Tell me about *Īmān* (faith)."

The Prophet ﷺ said:

"It is to believe in Allah, His angels, His books, His messengers, the Last Day, and to believe in divine destiny, the good and the bad of it."

He said: "You have spoken the truth."

He said: "Now tell me about *Iḥsān.*"

The Prophet ﷺ replied:

"It is to worship Allah as if you see Him. And even though you do not see Him, [know that] He sees you."

He then asked: "Tell me about the Hour."

The Prophet ﷺ said: "The one being asked does not know more than the one asking."

He said: "Then tell me about its signs."

The Prophet ﷺ replied:

"That the slave woman will give birth to her mistress, and that you will see the barefoot, naked, destitute shepherds competing in building tall structures."

Then the man left, and I remained seated for a while. Then the Prophet ﷺ said to me:

"O 'Umar, do you know who the questioner was?"

I said: "Allah and His Messenger know best."

He said: "That was Jibrīl. He came to teach you your religion." *(Hadith reported in Sahih Muslim, Book 1, Hadith 1)*

Chapter 30

THE QUR'AN HAS IT ALL

كِتَابٌ أَنزَلْنَاهُ إِلَيْكَ مُبَارَكٌ لِّيَدَّبَّرُوا آيَاتِهِ وَلِيَتَذَكَّرَ أُولُوا الْأَلْبَابِ

[This is] a blessed Book which We have revealed to you, [O Muhammad], that they might reflect upon its verses and that those of understanding would be reminded.

(*Sad* 38:29)

Through the chapters of this book, we have been on a journey to connect more deeply with the Qur'an. We have discovered answers to questions everyone thinks about in their daily lives. Some of these questions were about our purpose in this world, some were about practical concerns like food waste and dealing with money. Using the Qur'an as our lens on this world, we looked at our family life and relationships; at marriage, pregnancy and divorce. In the Qur'an we found Allah ﷻ addresses our feelings and defines for us the meaning of success and failure.

Qur'an has it all – Allah ﷻ tells us what He expects from us.

Our journey has not just been related to our worldly lives, but also what the Qur'an says about our afterlife-*akhirah* has been explored. From the moment we face death to receiving our book of deeds in front of Allah ﷻ, we found guidance on each of these subjects. Through understanding these verses, we've found that when we seek to understand, the Qur'an will guide us. It's now up to us to continue our relationship with Allah's ﷻ revelation, consistently turning to it, reading and pondering over its message.

The Qur'an as a light:

While we live in a fast-paced world full of distractions, people have access to an infinite amount of information, yet they are confused about their life, seeking answers. To find a way through this world, Allah ﷻ tells us that His book, the Qur'an is a light to guide us.

فَـَٔامِنُوا۟ بِٱللَّهِ وَرَسُولِهِۦ وَٱلنُّورِ ٱلَّذِىٓ أَنزَلْنَا ۚ وَٱللَّهُ بِمَا تَعْمَلُونَ خَبِيرٌ ۝

So believe in Allah, in His Messenger, and in the light We have sent down: Allah is fully aware of what you do.

(*al-Taghabun* 64: 8)

The Qur'an is the Word of Allah ﷻ and a gift we have been given that surpasses all other gifts. When we reflect on the fact that Allah ﷻ made us and guided us to Islam. He sent a Messenger ﷺ to put the Qur'an in action with his beautiful character. In this book, and through *Rasul Allah* ﷺ, Allah ﷻ has made everything we need to know clear, to reach *Jannah* and be amongst the righteous. In *Surah al-Isra*-The Night Journey, Allah ﷻ describes the relationship between the believer and the Qur'an:

إِنَّ هَٰذَا ٱلْقُرْءَانَ يَهْدِى لِلَّتِى هِىَ أَقْوَمُ وَيُبَشِّرُ ٱلْمُؤْمِنِينَ ٱلَّذِينَ يَعْمَلُونَ
ٱلصَّٰلِحَٰتِ أَنَّ لَهُمْ أَجْرًا كَبِيرًا ۝
وَأَنَّ ٱلَّذِينَ لَا يُؤْمِنُونَ بِٱلْءَاخِرَةِ أَعْتَدْنَا لَهُمْ عَذَابًا أَلِيمًا ۝

This Quran does indeed show the straightest way. It gives the faithful who do right the good news that they will have a great reward and warns that We have prepared an agonising punishment for those who do not believe in the world to come.

(*Bani Isra'il* 17:9-10)

Living with the Qur'an

Abu Umaamah al-Baahili ﷺ said: I heard the Messenger of Allah ﷺ say: "Read the Qur'an, for it will come on the Day of Resurrection and intercede for its companions…" (Muslim).

Each of us is at a different level of engaging with the Qur'an, and need to evaluate where we can make improvements. Do we need to read more consistently, until it is a daily habit? If we are reading regularly, are we taking time to do *taddabur* – contemplate on the message of the Qur'an? Do we need to find a *tafseer* class or resources to help us understand the meaning on a deeper level? Of equal importance is the question: are we putting what we learn into practise? If we make the effort to do this, we will by the Will of Allah ﷻ find our lives transformed, and hope for the best outcome in the hereafter.

When we live with the Qur'an, we are holding on to the rope of Allah ﷻ and are better connected as one body with the *ummah*. We ask Allah ﷻ to protect our brothers and sisters in Gaza, and all over the world where they are suffering and in need. May Allah ﷻ accept all their sacrifices and accept those who died as martyrs. May Allah ﷻ make it easy for those who lost members of their family and may they be rewarded abundantly.

May Allah ﷻ make the Qur'an the spring of our hearts, the light in our chests, the disappearance of our sadness, the remover of our worries and grief. May Allah ﷻ make us from the family of the Qur'an—those who recite its words, reflect over its meanings, internalise its wisdom, and act according to its guidance. May Allah ﷻ make us walking manifestations of the Qur'ans' morals, as was our beloved Messenger ﷺ.

Allāhumma Āmīn.